The 2500 Adages of Imam Ali

By

Imam Ali

Published by Left of Brain Books

Copyright © 2023 Left of Brain Books

ISBN 978-1-397-66511-9

First Edition

All rights reserved. No part of this publication may be reproduced, distributed, or transmitted in any form or by any means, including photocopying, recording, or other electronic or mechanical methods, without the prior written permission of the publisher, except in the case of brief quotations permitted by copyright law. Left of Brain Books is a division of Left Of Brain Onboarding Pty Ltd.

PUBLISHER'S PREFACE

About the Book

A collection of traditional sayings of Ali.

CONTENTS

PUBLISHER'S PREFACE
WORD OF THE TRANSLATOR 1
   WRITTEN FOR 3
   IMAM ALI (PUH) AND ELOQUENCE 4
   ADAGES OF IMAM ALI (PUH) IN NOBLE MANNERS 7
   ADAGES OF IMAM ALI (PUH) IN SOCIAL RELATIONS 63
   ADAGES OF IMAM ALI (PUH) IN MANNERS OF SPEECH AND SILENCE 67
   HIS ADAGES (PUH) ABOUT WISDOM AND WISE MEN, AND THE MIND AND THE MINDFUL MEN 73
   ADAGES OF IMAM ALI (PUH) ABOUT THE HUMAN NATURE 83
   ADAGES OF IMAM ALI (PUH) ABOUT VICEROYS AND RULERS 84
   ADAGES OF IMAM ALI (PUH) IN THE BAD HABITS AND AVOIDING THEM 88
   ADAGES OF IMAM ALI (PUH) IN SATIRIZING THE LIFE 122
   ADAGES OF IMAM ALI (PUH) IN CALLING FOR THE AFTER-LIFE 126
   HIS ADAGES (PUH) ABOUT RICHNESS, POVERTY AND MONEY 130
   POTIC ADAGES 133
   MOST IMPORTANT SOURCES OF THE BOOK 149

WORD OF THE TRANSLATOR

THIS is a humble translation for a book that can be considered modern, but the information it contains are of antiquity. This is the book of "2500 adages for imam Ali (puh)." The book might not contain exactly that number of adages but it might be some number around that.

The book categorizes the adages and sayings in different chapters, each contain a specific branch of life. At the end of the book, there is the "poetic adages" which I have translated without keeping the rhyme, but meaning, as much as possible. The main translations are taken by meanings and not by translating word for word method, for there are different obstacles that are not avoidable in this way.

A little introduction might be useful to know who is imam Ali (puh). Imam Ali is the cousin of prophet Mohammed (puh), and as Shiites believe, he is the rightful successor and leader to be after the death of prophet Mohammed (puh). But unfortunately, his rights are taken from him and later he became in what is called "Islamic History" to be the fourth caliph for Muslims at that time, ending the period known as the time of "Al-Kholafa' Al-Rashideen" (The guided caliphs). The event of his rule and his rights and what happened to him after the prophet's death is still shrouded with dark clouds, and it is still the main course of debate among the two main branches of Islam, Shia and Sunni.

In this translation I preferred to use the word "Allah" instead of "God" because "God" has also another word in Arabic.
My own comments and understanding of some phrases are enclosed by "[ ]," while explanations or further translations are enclosed by "( )." The abbreviation "puh" is the short form of "peace upon him," which is a frequently used phrase by Muslims for dignify a holy person. However, some other phrases can be fit to be translations to this after all.

I hope you enjoy the deep meanings in this books and I hope that the obstacle of the language put down and get the benefits from the wisdom mentioned in these coming lines.

WRITTEN FOR

In the name of Allah, the Beneficent, the Merciful

To

TO the garden of wisdom that had grown up and flooded, and flooded, to the wise man whose tongue bled with abundant wisdom, to him whose adages and sermons lighted up from his honourable mouth like pearly drops.

To the one who filled life with his wisdom, and hugged the minds, the minds of his companions, and delivered them to the wider upper fields, I mean knowledge.

To the one who enriched the Arabic language with his eloquent speech.

To the master of eloquent ones and the prince of the wise men.

To the prince of believers

To him...

I raise this little of what was collected from the pearls of his wisdom and the magnificent of his sermons.

IMAM ALI (PUH) AND ELOQUENCE

THE talk about imam Ali (puh) is branched to many fields, for every field of virtues, he (puh) was the first to indulge himself into it, and what such few pages would do to talk about him and about his many virtues, and it is enough to be taken as a clue, the speech of Ibn Abbaas, the rabbi of this nation with his knowledge, and it is narrated that a man asked Ibn Abbaas and said: how many are the virtues of Ali ben Abi Taalib, and I think they are 3,000... Then said Ibn Abbaas: It is closer to 30,000 more than 3,000; and then he said: if trees were made into pens and the sea into an ink and humans and djinns were writers and calculators, they will never count the virtues of the prince of believers (puh).

But for the wisdom the says, what cannot be reached all, its partitions are not to be left, and who missed the abundance should take what is left over, we are here seeking to show some of the eloquence that the imam had, to be an introduction to read this book, which contains pearls and wonderful things from the adages of the imam, that stand as a clue for his long experience in this field.

Eloquence:

And before speaking about the eloquence of the imam (puh), we must stop with eloquence and its definition, in language and in general.

Ibn Mandhoor defines eloquence as to be the purity of language, and adds in his speech about the eloquent man: the good speech is its purest, and reaches by the phrase of the tongue, the interior of what is in the heart.

Sheikh Al-Torayhi expands what Ibn Mandhoor said, and makes a condition for the eloquent speech on 3 terms: the correctness of the language, and a coincidence to the desired meaning, and truthfulness in the soul.

In general, it is obvious that the eloquent speech is the purity of the talk and its shortness, or what achieves the meaning in the closest way, and eloquence in the speech includes all the types of speeches, from speeches and prose and poetry and thoughts and sermons...etc.

And here we will encounter only the adages and the sermons, some of them which came in form of a poetry or as a prose, for both of them are one, for poetry in its shape and style, is not what charms the minds, but it is what it carries of eternal meanings.

The wise saying, is born from the experience and meditating and conclusion, and it is a phase that passed over the level of the childhood of the thought and its youth to the level of its old age; on the other hand, the sermons coincide with adages for they are the result of meditating and experimenting, but they are special because they are specialized for inviting people for the after-life and hating the finite life.

Eloquence of the imam; Adages as an Example
* The facts that affected his adages:

Maybe one of the most obvious things that affected the adages of the imam, is the religion of Islam, and mainly the book of Allah that was revealed, that is Quran. For Quran is the topmost in eloquence and purity in language, and it is enough as a clue for this, how the eloquent speakers of Arabs stood up surprised in front of the greatness of its own eloquence, while they are the great owners of literature and the giants of thought and eloquence.

Adding to that, the imam had a noble soul and did not accept to see the people under humiliation. These characters are encouraged by Islam, thus the imam (puh) went on starting from his own self and feeding his thought with the teachings of Islam, he went on to build a unique community depending on unique ideas that he (puh) explained in his adages and his speeches.

Types of adages and their subjects: the adages of imam Ali (puh) included the different fields of life, like religion, community, manners, sermons and politics.

And they are considered adages because they are general and applicable for every place and time, and the clue for this is, is how they persisted with time, as a live witness for how great is the imam.

Their characteristics and specialities: the adages of imam Ali (puh) are full with meanings of style and alive with the spirit of sincerity and belief, and alloyed in a block of stylized expression, so much that Abbaas Mahmood Al-Aqqaad [a modern writer and author] said in his book Abqariyatul-Imam (The Ingenuity of the Imam): They are (the adages) more eloquent in expression and has an abundance in beauty of the speech.

Testimonies About The Eloquence of the Imam:

- Abdul-Hameed Al-Kaatib said: I memorized seventy speeches from the speeches of the bald man, and they flooded me and flooded me again. [The bald man was a title used by the enemies of imam Ali (puh) as to mock at him].

- His eloquence even attracted his fierce enemy, Mo'awiyah, when he said, when Mahnaf ben Abi-Mahnaf said to him: I came to you from the sickest of people, and he answered him: Woe to you! how come he is the sickest of people! by Allah no one spread the eloquence for Quraish [the tribe of the prophet] except of him.

But after all the most truthful witness in all of that, is how these adages persisted all the time, despite the many enemies of the imam, no one dared to mention them with badness.

Ahmad Ali Dakheel

ADAGES OF IMAM ALI (PUH) IN NOBLE MANNERS

1. Satisfaction is an infinite money.

2. Toleration and patience are twins produced by the high determination.

3. Toleration is a clan.

4. Piety is the head of all manners.

5. Chastity is the ornament of poverty, and giving thanks is the ornament of richness.

6. Be good to the lineage of others, thus you will be saved with your lineages.

7. If you feared poverty, then trade with Allah by charity.

8. Generosity is more passionate than close relations.

9. It is enough for satisfaction to be a kingdom, and with good manners to be a delight.

10. He who shyness bestowed upon him its veil, people would not see his flaws.

11. Reveal down the fortune by giving charity.

12. He shall not be in need, he who saved.

13. Being straight is safety.

14. The patience, is the head of the faith.

15. Justice, is the title of Nobility.

16. Justice, is the virtue of the human being.

17. Humility raises the low one.

18. The best of manners is that of the generosity.

19. From generosity comes the best of manners.

20. All the (high) lineage shall be ended, except for the mind and the good manners.

21. Take over the patience, for it is the fruit of wisdom.

22. It is of determination to memorize the experiment.

23. Be satisfied (with yourself) and you shall be exalted.

24. No honour is higher than faith.

25. No living is better than the good manners.

26. Truth is the garment of religion (faith).

27. No work greater than being pious.

28. Asceticism is the fruit of believing.

29. Faith is not useful without piety.

30. He who is just, shall be able. [Able here means someone who is depended on and reliable with expanded authority].

31. Be depending (on Allah) and you shall be satisfied.

32. Work and you shall save.

33. Honour is not complete unless with generosity and humility.

34. No faith is like shyness and humility.

35. Cheerfulness is a sign of the free man.

36. No faith for him, he who does not avoid. [Avoid here means protecting oneself when possible for the sake of keeping on with the faith instead of being pressed to change it].

37. Giving thanks is the fort of favours.

38. Asceticism is the best of garments.

39. No winning for him who does not have patience.

40. Asceticism is the best companion.

41. No protection for him who have no faith.

42. Forgiving is the address of nobility.

43. No faith for him who does not believe. [Believe here means the absolute trust in God].

44. Giving favours is the zakat (almsgiving) of the favours.

45. Truth is the best way.

46. Asceticism is the character of the loyal ones.

47. No safety for him who have no faith.

48. The smart one is him who shortened his hopes.

49. Being loyal is the honour that remains. [Loyal here means being loyal to God].

50. The faith of someone keeps him away from every low-deed.

51. No reward for him who has no work to do.

52. Be respectful for your elders, thus may your youngsters be respectful toward you.

53. The asceticism of one man is according to the level of his faith.

54. No honour unless by being loyal. [see 49].

55. It is one of the best companions, that is the faith.

56. Accompanying those of virtues, is a life.

57. One thing is essential for being faithful, that is to keep away from sins.

58. He shall not be overwhelmed, who takes truth as a clue.

59. Fighting the lusts of the self is an address of nobility.

60. Living with the faithful ones, verily brings the honour.

61. It is one of the characteristics of the faithful to have altruism.

62. He shall not be surprised when adversity comes, who is affirm.

63. Monotheism is the life of the soul.

64. Depending (on Allah) is the fort of wisdom.

65. With repentance, the forgiveness shall be.

66. The completeness of the virtues, is to have the good manners.

67. The wise man is not independent of consulting.

68. Who gave goodness shall find it.

69. As you have mercy, mercy shall be taken upon you.

70. Who his deeds turned good, he shall what he desires from Allah.

71. He shall not be fought against who takes truth as a clue.

72. Who hated evil shall be infallible.

73. Be true and you shall be loyal.

74. Who feared Allah, Allah shall protect him.

75. Goodness is not useful without smartness.

76. Who says the truth shall survive.

77. Be a believer and you shall be strong.

78. Who mentions Allah a lot, his mind shall be enlightened.

79. Be faithful and you shall be pure.

80. No way for safety except by truth.

81. Who turns victorious for the truth gains a lot.

82. Be one of a sweet patience at the time of the bitter matters.

83. Who neglects (the bad) shall give relief to his heart.

84. No good way except of being faith.

85. Forgiveness is the crown of virtues.

86. No safe way except of the straight way.

87. The one who avoids evil is like the doer of goodness.

88. The honour of the determination is the doing of goodness.

89. The adage is a healing advice.

90. Adversities are not perishable unless by patience.

91. Of the signs of virtues, the early rewards. [meaning giving rewards for some deed before it is completely over].

92. Passion leads to peace.

93. No messenger is more obvious than the truth.

94. It is a part of happiness to be able to do the good things.

95. Generosity is the veil of the flaws.

96. The key to win is to have patience.

97. Who thanks a lot, his favours shall be a lot.

98. Favour is with charity.

99. The key to the good is to perish the evil.

100. Be a fighter for your lusts and a seeker for your survival.

101. The survival is with the faith.

102. Who had been good to his parents, his children shall be good toward him.

103. No greater favour there is, more than being successful.

104. Whose intention was good, success would provide him.

105. Be generous with truth and parsimonious with mischief.

106. No honour higher than tolerance.

107. Determination is firmness.

108. Satisfaction is enough as a fortune.

109. Who struggled to achieve justice, verily he shall success.

110. No supply like faith.

111. It is of generosity to satisfy the promises.

112. It is enough for consulting to be as a support.

113. He who believed, shall do the good.

114. No companion like the good manner.

115. Who spends his money, shall own the necks of people. [meaning spending money in good ways makes good people always owe to that person].

116. Who stepped aside shall be safe. [Stepping aside here means being away from useless ornamentations of this life and away from useless struggles and competitions].

117. No struggle like the struggle against the lusts of oneself.

118. It is one of the best companions of faith, that is shyness.

119. Who gives many a charity, is beloved by his brethren.

120. Who knew, would be satisfied.

121. Who got away from people, he shall be happy with Allah the Exalted.

122. It is enough for humility to be an honour.

123. It is of the best supplies, that is the good deeds.

124. Who got satisfied with himself, that will lead him to chastity.

125. it is enough for tolerance to be as respect.

126. Who has the habit of being just, then he shall reach the places of nobility.

127. Fighting against the lusts of oneself is the best of fights.

128. Nothing fixed the faith like piety.

129. Who knew Allah, shall never be miserable.

130. It is of the best treasures, that is being loyal.

131. No piety like stopping illegal deeds.

132. No worshipping like doing the daily duties. [Daily duties here mean the things that are a must for a muslim, like praying the 5 daily prayers and fasting in the month of Ramadhan and other things].

133. He who consults Allah (Istikharah) shall never regret. [Istikhara is the Arabic word and sometimes used in translations in this field. It means to ask God for guidance in some matters where hesitations take place].

134. He who fears no one, shall never fear.

135. No faith like patience.

136. It is of the best habits, that is the satisfaction.

137. He shall not astray, he who consults.

138. One of the expiations of the great sins, is to help the needy.

139. No supply like tolerance.

140. Whose speech was true, his clue shall be granted (correct).

141. It is enough for believing to be as a worship.

142. No tolerance like forgiveness.

143. He who becomes patient, shall never be hurt.

144. Who thanked Allah, He shall make him rich.

145. Who lives with people in peace shall be safe.

146. No gain like the reward (of Allah).

147. It is of the dignity of the soul, to hold on the satisfaction.

148. He who consults the men, shared their minds.

149. He who did his best in good deeds, his mention shall raise.

150. Struggling (against lust) is bounded to the heart (feelings).

151. No advice like warning.

152. It is of the best faith, that is the good manners.

153. He who gets scared of he punishment, shall be away from the sins.

154. For every good deed there is a reward.

155. Whose honour was dignified, then money is cheap for him.

156. No worship like thinking (meditation).

157. He is guided who obeyed his God and feared his sin.

158. It is of the best weapons, that is praying (Dua').

159. How many hard things that gets easy with passion.

160. How many a low class man got raised by his good manners.

161. No thought like planning.

162. It is one of the best ways (to get things done), that is obeying (Allah).

163. Every one satisfied (for what he has) is in relief.

164. Who has many a charity, his servants and helpers are many.

165. In mentioning (the name of Allah), there lies the life of hearts.

166. It is the best supply, that is patience at the time of adversity.

167. Who uses passion, reveals the fortune.

168. Satisfying Allah, that is the ultimate goal.

169. In obeying (Allah) lie the treasures of gains.

170. He who stopped at his limit (level), shall be dignified by the people.

171. It is a good supply that is the favour-doing.

172. With giving thanks, the favours last. [The favours meant here are those bestowed by God].

173. How good is being generous while in need.

174. Who believed Allah, he shall be safe.

175. Let your manners be the generosity and doing the good.

176. It is a good gift, that is the advice.

177. With asceticism, wisdom bears fruit.

178. How good it is to forgive while you are able. [Able means able to return the harm or take revenge].

179. He who advises himself, is better to advise others.

180. He who obeyed his imam, then he obeyed his God.

181. In fighting against the will of the soul, there lies the completeness of goodness.

182. It is a good worship, that is fearing. [Fearing means fearing God all the time].

183. With sincerity, the deeds are raised.

184. Necks are not enslaved by something, like they do for the good deed.

185. He who asks for victory from Allah, his victory shall be a high one.

186. In good manners lie the treasures of fortunes.

187. He who watches the endings, shall be safe from the adversities.

188. Be kind and do not be a squanderer.

189. It is a good manner, that is being calm.

190. With faith, the work bears fruit.

191. Favours (of Allah) are not protected with such a thing, like giving thanks.

192. In consulting lies the core of guidance.

193. In opposing the soul, lies its guidance.

194. He who understood, shall be kind.

195. The jealousy of a man is faith.

196. Being connected to the relatives, that is the grower of favours and the banisher of adversities.

197. He who degrades himself, shall be highly raised.

198. Take the way of chastity, for it is the best companion.

199. If love is in the right place, then it is because of peaceful time.

200. The cure of the soul is to be less greedy.

201. He who has been just, shall be taken with just.

202. Neglecting the bad is a habit of nobility.

203. Neglecting the bad is the most noble act of faith.

204. tightening the kinship is the best of manners of the generous ones.

205. He who takes patience shall win.

206. The habit of the generous people is to do the goodness.

207. To gain the win of paradise, it is to fight against the lust of the self.

208. The man is truthful according to the level of his nobility.

209. He who conquers his lust shall be dignified.

210. The veil of flaws, generosity and chastity.

211. Doing good, that is the ornament of man.

212. The chest of the man is the chest of his secrets. [Chest in the beginning means the area of the body of a man].

213. He who obeys Allah shall win.

214. You should mention Allah, for He is the light of heart.

215. He who is generous shall conquer.

216. He who is satisfied (with himself) is a rich one.

217. Keeping kinship, reveals the favours and banishes the adversities.

218. Keeping kinship, grows the numbers and bears fruit for the favours.

219. He who spends his money (in goodness) shall be raised (in status).

220. You should be satisfied, in hard times and the easy ones.

221. Keeping the kinship, grows the numbers and applies success.

222. He who becomes kind, shall be dignified.

223. The winning of the generous one is a survival.

224. The charity giving in public, prevents the bad end.

225. He who is humble shall be raised.

226. Take care of loyalty, for it is the strongest shield.

227. The work is good as long the intention is good.

228. He who has been loyal shall reach the hopes.

229. The purpose (goal) of surrender (to Allah), is to win the Place of Favours (paradise, heavens).

230. Diet, is the fix of the body.

231. He who prevents, shall be safe.

232. He shall gain the goodness who asks for it.

233. The fix of religion is asceticism.

234. He who gives favours shall be served.

235. Doing the good deeds is a virtue for the human being.

236. He who shall be victorious to the truth, shall win.

237. The extreme of good manners, that is altruism.

238. He who dealt with others in a passionate way, shall win.

239. The title of nobility, is to deal with people by good deeds.

240. He who works with the truth is a survival.

241. In keeping the kinship lies the guardian of favours.

242. He who accepted destiny, shall have a relief.

243. The determination to do the goodness turns off the fire of evil.

244. He who asks shall gain the benefit.

245. Live along with people of virtues and you shall be happy and a noble.

246. He who becomes generous shall conquer.

247. The title of mindfulness. is to care about people.

248. Who uses the truth as a clue, he shall feel the coldness. [Coldness here is a figurative speech referring to the effect of happiness when it comes to the heart].

249. The purpose of the struggle (Jihad) is that one should fight himself (against lusts).

250. He who becomes patient shall get what he desires.

251. In surrendering (to Allah) lies the faith.

252. He who depended (on Allah) shall never care.

253. In giving thanks for the favours, these favours shall last.

254. He who advised you, rescued you.

255. In generosity lies the loveliness.

256. He who mentions Allah, Allah shall mention him.

257. In every good deed lies a reward.

258. He who struggles against himself, completed his own piety.

259. The keeper of a secret is a loyal and a trustee.

260. Who works with the truth shall succeed.

261. Blessedness for him, who watches his God and feared his sin.

262. He who judges himself shall win.

263. Consult those of the mind and you shall be safe from mistake.

264. Who protected himself (against sins) shall be respected.

265. You should give thanks (to Allah) whether in adversity or good time.

266. He who disobeyed the lust of himself, he mended it (himself).

267. The mend of the soul is to struggle against the lust.

268. He who becomes patient, his adversity shall become low.

269. The honour of the man is his just, and his beauty is his nobility.

270. He who repents then depended (on Allah).

271. Blessedness is for him who keeps the obedience of his God.

272. Who regretted then he had repented.

273. The reason for loveliness is generosity.

274. He who knows life, shall abstain from it.

275. The mend of religion (faith) is by the true believing.

276. He who takes refuge unto Allah, He shall rescue him.

277. The reason for loveliness is loyalty.

278. Who depended on Allah, He shall make him satisfied.

279. You should be calm, for it is the best ornament.

280. He who spends his money (in goodness) shall enslave.

281. The honour of the faithful is his faith, and his glory is his obedience.

282. He who spends his fortune (in goodness) shall be thanked.

283. The lords of heavens are the pious and faithful.

284. He who takes patience, his adversity shall come low.

285. Do the charities, and then you shall be safe from the lewdness of parsimony.

286. He who takes parsimony for his religion shall be exalted. [meaning, he who holds tight on his religion (not for money) should be exalted].

287. Be peaceful with people and your life shall be safe.

288. Who works rightly shall gain.

289. Blessedness shall be for him who made his heart feel the faith.

290. He who knew himself (correctly), knew his God.

291. The ladder of nobility is humility and generosity.

292. He who had been good to his neighbours, his servants shall be abundant.

293. Over truth and sincerity, faith shall be built.

294. Charity is a successful cure.

295. He who keeps away (from people), his faith shall be mended.

296. The reason for fixing the religion is piety.

297. He who gains the kindness, his recklessness shall be put down.

298. Blessedness for him, who kept the way of obedience for his God.

299. he who got satisfied with destiny, shall live blessed.

300. Two things, their rewards cannot be weighed: Forgiveness and Justice.

301. Be kind, for it is a manner that is accepted.

302. He who left his matters to Allah shall succeed.

303. Be peaceful with people and you shall be in peace, and work for the after-life and you shall win.

304. He who was guided by the guidance of Allah shall be guided by Allah.

305. The reason behind a good faith, piety.

306. He who loaned Allah (did the good for the sake of Allah), shall be rewarded by Him.

307. Blessedness for him, whose tongue was busy with the mention (of Allah).

308. He who asks Allah, He shall give him what he asks.

309. The reason behind respect, kindness.

310. He who keeps himself away from begging shall be exalted.

311. You should be addicted to work, in time of activity or laziness.

312. The peaceful living lies in taking care of people.

313. He who keeps his promises shall be a loyal one.

314. Two things are part of religion (faith): Truth and Belief.

315. He who owns his own lusts, shall be pious.

316. The reason behind authority, generosity.

317. He who owns his own anger, shall be kind.

318. Blessedness for him, who raced over his fate and did his work with sincerity.

319. He who owned his mind is a wise man.

320. The reason behind the goodness of the self is piety.

321. He who asks when he is young, shall answer when he is old.

322. Be sincere, for it is the best of the faith.

323. He who kept away from people, protected his faith.

324. He who has the good manners, shall have the wide fortune.

325. Blessedness for him, who fears Allah and remained safe.

326. The law of the generous is to keep their promises.

327. He whose interior was good, his apparent part shall be good.

328. The thanks giving of the believer, appears in his works.

329. The weapon of the believer is praying for forgiveness.

330. He who gets exaltation from Allah, no ruler can put him down.

331. According to the level of the nobility, comes the level of generosity.

332. The worship becomes fixed by depending (on Allah).

333. He who takes refuge unto Allah, no ruler can hurt him.

334. The weapon of the believer, the prayers (Dua').

335. He who seeks peace, should keep on straight.

336. According to the level of shyness, the chastity shall be.

337. The mend of religion (faith) is by the good belief.

338. He who is always true, shall never be prohibited from dignity.

339. The habit of the noble ones, generosity.

340. Blessedness for him, who remembered the after-life and made the good.

341. He who works for the after-life, shall win the success.

342. The happiness of someone is in satisfaction (about what one got).

343. He who has satisfaction in what Allah had given him, he is verily a rich one.

344. The obedience of the guidance shall rescue oneself.

345. He who trusts Allah, shall depend on Him.

346. No dependant (on Allah) has any tiresome times.

347. He who has a strong faith, his sincerity is high.

348. The seed of faith is to read Quran.

349. Blessedness for the soul, that did for its God what He had assigned to it.

350. He who believed in the reward, shall do the goodness.

351. He is certainly a victorious one, who depended on patience for victory.

352. Running after manners, is the beauty of one's lineage.

353. The zakat (almsgiving) of beauty, should be chastity.

354. No one shall win paradise unless he is running after it.

355. He is exalted who is satisfied (with what he has).

356. The good after-life lies in the good work.

357. No one shall receive the rewards of goodness except of him who does it.

358. Giving thanks to the Giver, is a shield against adversities.

359. He is verily awake who takes lessons (from life).

360. The zakat (almsgiving) of fortune, is to give (some of) it.

361. Jealousy comes according to the level of protection.

362. Thanking God, shall reveal the favours.

363. According to the level of the honour of the self shall be the level of nobility.

364. Having patience for a long time is a character of the faithful people.

365. The mend to the mind, that is manners.

366. The hearer of the mention of Allah, is a mentioner.

367. The zakat (almsgiving) of bravery is to fight on the way of Allah.

368. The ornament of faith is piety.

369. Banishing away the lust, is a character of wise people.

370. The ornament of worshipping is humility.

371. The head of the faith is truthfulness.

372. The ornament of wisdom is giving away for this life.

373. The head of Islam is sincerity.

374. The increment in ignorance lowers down.

375. The satisfaction of Allah, is the closest thing one can achieve.

376. The satisfaction of Allah is bound to obedience towards Him.

377. The head of wisdom is to be bound to the truth.

378. The head of faith is patience.

379. The mercy toward the weak people reveals down the mercy.

380. The head of piety is to neglect the bad things (in people).

381. The head of piety is to let go of lust.

382. The head of kindness is to hold on the anger.

383. The head of foreseeing is meditation.

384. The one who mentions Allah is like one who sits with Him.

385. The mention of Allah shall banish away the devil.

386. The mention of Allah is the cure of those of sick souls.

387. The mention of Allah shall banish diseases and misery.

388. The clue to a man's faith is his piety.

389. The clue to a man's jealousy is his chastity.

390. The best of works is to have an equal amount of fear and hope.

391. Go deep into the depths wherever truth is.

392. Fearing Allah is the wing of faith.

393. Take determination and be bound to wisdom, and then the endings shall be fine.

394. Fearing Allah brings to the fearer the feeling of safety.

395. Fear Allah so that He makes you safe, and do not feel safe towards Him and so He might punish you.

396. The sweetness of the winning, clears the bitterness of patience.

397. The noble of all the manners, loyalty.

398. The nobility if someone is his wisdom, and his beauty lies in his brain (mind).

399. Remembering the experiments, this is the head of mind (wisdom).

400. The result of humility, the honour.

401. The sadness of hearts, clears the sins.

402. The good thanks giving, allows more increments.

403. The good manners is the best of faith.

404. Be a neighbour for wise men (scholars) and you shall be enlightened. [Be a neighbour here means simply to be with them whenever possible].

405. The reason for the good faith, the good belief.

406. The fight against anger with kindness, that is an evidence for nobility.

407. The good kindness is an evidence for the abundant wisdom.

408. Fighting against the lusts of the self with science (wisdom), that is an address of the mindfulness.

409. The good intention comes from the good inner self.

410. The rewards of an adversity come according to how much patience was taken for it.

411. The good establishment is the best leader.

412. The good chastity is one of the characters of the nobles.

413. The beauty of good doings, is to leave mentioning the favours. [Mentioning favours here means to remind someone about the favours that was done to him as to humiliate him or press on him].

414. Being in good satisfaction is part of chastity.

415. The beauty of a favour is to complete it.

416. The goodness of understanding is a title of piety.

417. The beauty of the intention is a reason for reaching the goal.

418. The good patience owns every matter.

419. The beauty of the free man is to avoid the shame.

420. The good patience is the step to the victory.

421. Give what is finite and you shall win the infinite.

422. The good cheerfulness is a character of every free man.

423. The fight against the lusts of the self is the dowry of paradise.

424. The good ask for forgiveness clears the sins.

425. The beauty of the believer lies in his faith.

426. The good manners are the head of every good deed.

427. Sit with the wise men and you shall be happy.

428. The good manners are a clue for the generous lineage.

429. The beauty of a man lies in respectfulness.

430. The good reputation (of someone) is a clue for the good inner self (of that one).

431. The collection of goodness lies in the works of goodness.

432. The beauty of faith lies in piety.

433. The beauty of the intention is an evidence of the purity of birth.

434. Sit with the kind people and you shall increase your kindness.

435. Sit with the wise men and you shall increase your wisdom.

436. The guest of goodness is a favour (from Allah).

437. The garment of piety is the noblest of all garments.

438. The garment of health is the most blessed of all garments.

439. Your garments on others shall stay more than they do on you.

440. Be generous with what you find and you shall be thanked.

441. The price of paradise is the good deeds.

442. The rewards of patience shall erase the bitterness of adversity.

443. The rewards of Jihad is the greatest of all rewards.

444. The rewards of patience is the highest of all rewards.

445. The humility of someone shall raise him up.

446. The completeness of nobility is humility.

447. Make your weighs heavier with the good deeds.

448. The complete success is to start with the good works.

449. The stability of faith depends on the might of belief.

450. To release in a hurry, this is success. ["To release" here has several meanings, but most probably the imam meant to release a woman in cases of divorce when a couple find out it's not possible to live with each other. Some men might take this chance to hurt the woman in any manner, while noble people release the woman with dignity, and this is what might be the meaning of the imam's saying. The meaning closest to this context can be found out in Quran, 2:231. Check].

451. Make your weights heavier with charity. [The weights meant here are not those of the body but the weights of the good deeds or the bad deeds recorded in the life of the human being and by which he/she shall be judged for in the after-life].

452. To hurry up with mending, that is a reform.

453. The fruit of faith, is winning before Allah. [Before = in front of].

454. Be a trader with Allah and you shall win.

455. The fruit of firmness is safety.

456. The fruit of faith, sincerity.

457. The crown of the man is his chastity, and his ornament is his justice.

458. The fruit of believing, asceticism.

459. The early times of Saturday and Thursday are blessed.

460. The fruit of repentance is to catch up the flaws of the soul.

461. The bless of money lies in charity giving.

462. The fruit of judging the self, soul mending.

463. To give from the fortune, that is the zakat (almsgiving) of the fortune. [Zakat means the process by which money is purified].

464. The fruit of believing, is the desire to stay in the eternal place.

465. To leave the lusts, this is the best of worshipping and the most beautiful of habits.

466. The fruit of wisdom is to win.

467. To be good to the parents, this is the greatest assigned task.

468. The fruit of satisfaction (with what one has), dignity.

469. Bring to yourself that good tidings of success and winning, if you were patient.

470. The fruit of asceticism is the justice.

471. Race to do the good deeds, for they are an opportunity.

472. The fruit of chastity, satisfaction.

473. The bless of age lies in the good deeds.

474. The fruit of piety, the happiness in this life and the after-life.

475. The cry of the slave for the fear of Allah, shall clears his sins.

476. The fruit of the mention (of Allah), the enlightenment of hearts.

477. Avoid the sins that Allah prohibited and you shall succeed.

478. The fruit of giving thanks, the increment in (given) favours.

479. Be optimistic about the good things and you shall succeed.

480. The fruit of generosity, the tightening of kinship.

481. To do the favour in a hurry, that is the owning of the favour.

482. To do the good deed in a hurry, that is an increment in the good deeds.

483. To do the salutations (first), that is from the good manners and habits.

484. Bear (be patient), and you shall be honoured.

485. Take the chance (while you can) before it becomes something you can't swallow.

486. If a man tightens his kinships, that is a charity.

487. If you owned, then be passionate.

488. Do the obedience in the early times and you shall be happy.

489. If you are given then give thanks.

490. Do the good in an early time and you shall be guided.

491. If you are in an adversity, be patient.

492. Your cheerfulness is the beginning of your good deeds, and your promise is the beginning of your giving.

493. If you shall punish, then be passionate.

494. Be the first to do the obedience and you shall be happy.

495. If you did a favour, then keep it a secret.

496. Be the first to do the goodness and you shall be guided.

497. If a favour was done to you, then spread it.

498. By giving thanks, the favours last.

499. If you praised (someone) then make it short.

500. By being humble, thus comes the honour.

501. If you are given then give.

502. By giving the favours, the levels are raised.

503. If you are wronged, then forgive.

504. By respect, dignity grows.

505. If you are not given, then be satisfied.

506. By kindness, allies grow.

507. If you made brothers, then be generous to the right of brotherhood. [Made brothers in this context means to fix the relation between two persons].

508. By guidance, enlightenment increases.

509. If you did a favour our of a favour, then you did give the thanks for it.

510. By altruism, free men are enslaved.

511. If you did a sin, then regret for it.

512. By good deeds, the human being is enslaved.

513. If the exalted one got insight into the matters of religion, then he has been humble.

514. By sermons, the ignorance shall be banished.

515. If the low one thought deeply into the religion's laws, he shall be raised.

516. By humility, the nobility is measured.

517. If the manners were good, then the words are to be gentle.

518. By endearment, love should be.

519. If sincerity was strong, then truth shall be abundant.

520. By the ability to do the good work, lies the happiness.

521. If the mind was complete, the love of lust will wane.

522. By generosity, authority should be.

523. If you see the goodness, then take its lead.

524. By believing, worshipping is complete.

525. The safest of matters' end, that is the end of patience.

526. By passion, courage is complete.

527. If you ask for dignity, then ask for it in obedience (to Allah).

528. By the adversities, paradise is won.

529. You stand up with your manners, thus decorate it with kindness.

530. By patience, the adversity shall be lowered down.

531. If you worked for the after-life then verily you have won.

532. By faith, survival shall be.

533. If you were humble, Allah will raise you up.

534. By health, the beauty of life is founded.

535. If you leave the sins, then Allah will love you.

536. By mentioning Allah, the favour shall be revealed.

537. If you believed in Allah, then your end is to be good.

538. By faith, one shall find the good ones. [Good ones here is not clear in Arabic, whether it would be the good deeds, or the good women as well! But most probably it is the deeds meant here].

539. If you feared Allah, He shall protect you.

540. By the good deeds, the free man is owned.

541. If you made yourself respected, you shall be dignified.

542. By controlling the wrath, kindness shall be.

543. If you made peace with Allah, then you shall be safe and win.

544. By saying the truth, survival shall be.

545. If Allah wanted to do good to one of His slaves, He shall keep his abdomen and honour clean of disgrace.

546. By saying the truth, courage is completed.

547. Firmness is, to obey Allah and refuse the self.

548. By patience, goals shall be easy.

549. Generosity is to go away from the sins.

550. By patience, the goals are reached.

551. Nobility is to be high over the disgrace.

552. By asceticism, wisdom shall bear fruit.

553. The lords of this life and the after-life are the generous ones.

554. By giving, the necks are enslaved.

555. Faith, is to clean oneself from the sins.

556. By passion, the goals are reached.

557. Generosity is to give the most desired things, and being hospitable to the seeker.

558. By chastity, the works are purified.

559. He whom is covered by the veil of shyness, people will not see his flaws.

560. By praying, the adversity is banished away.

561. He who takes the steps of determination, shall be dignified by the nations.

562. For the good deeds, the praise is good.

563. You are judged for your deeds, thus do the good deeds.

564. By sincerity, the deeds are raised.

565. If you have given yourself to Allah, then your self is safe.

566. By satisfaction (with what one has) shall be dignity.

567. If Allah has given you some favours, then give thanks.

568. By patience, the high matters shall be reachable.

569. If Allah tried you with an adversity then be patient.

570. By faith, one shall be raised above the low things.

571. If you were patient, the pen (of destiny) shall run over you and you will be rewarded.

572. By the good manners, the fortunes are revealed.

573. The best of jihad (struggle) is that of a man against his own self.

574. By the good works, one finds the faith.

575. If you just be patient, then Allah shall find for you in every adversity a compensation.

576. By the originality of the opinion, the firmness stands up.

577. The best of wisdom, being calm and kind.

578. By jihad, the soul is fixed.

579. To start the greetings, that is one of the best manners.

580. By forgiving, mercy is revealed.

581. It is a favour that one cannot proceed with sins.

582. By repentance, sins are cleared.

583. By piety, the deeds are purified.

584. Believers are verily fearful (of Allah).

585. Yourselves got prices, so do not sell them for something less than paradise.

586. By giving much, the generous one is known.

587. If you see a wronged person, then help him against the wrong-doer.

588. By how much he can bear, the kind person is known.

589. If Allah chooses to raise a slave, then He shall inspire him with faith.

590. By doing the good, the free men are to be owned.

591. If Allah shall be generous to someone, He then shall make him busy with His love.

592. By keeping the promises, the pious ones are known.

593. If you shall avoid, then avoid what Allah prohibited.

594. By the good obedience, the good people are known.

595. If the pious one escaped away from the people, then seek after him.

596. By faith, the believer is purified.

597. If Allah is to choose a slave, He shall then put on him the veil of fear (of Him).

598. By forgiveness, the glory is made great.

599. If a favour was revealed upon you, then make its reply to be thanks giving.

600. By giving, the praise shall increase.

601. If Allah loved a slave, then He shall inspire him with truthfulness.

602. By giving, the flaws are veiled.

603. If Allah is to be generous with a slave, He shall help him to establish the truth.

604. By keeping the kinship, the favours are to be revealed.

605. Kindness is to control the wrath and owning the soul. [owning the soul means to control the lust].

606. By enlightenment, one shall understand.

607. If Allah is to love a slave, He shall inspire him with the good worshipping.

608. Keeping the promises is part of faith.

609. The good deed which has the fastest response in return is, to be good (toward others).

610. The wisest of people is he who looks into the ends (of matters).

611. The safest of matters, is the reward of patience.

612. The best of the manners of men is that of kindness.

613. The best of truth, is that of keeping the promise.

614. The best of rewards is that of justice.

615. The best of generosity is to do the best (for others).

616. The most honourable of sayings is that of the truth.

617. The best of faith is the shortening of hope. [shortening of hope means someone should not hang all his life on one hope which might cause his life to be ruined in one way or another].

618. The most noble lineage, is that of the manners.

619. The best of honour, is that of doing the good.

620. The highest of worshipping is that of doing a work sincerely.

621. The best of faith, is to be have the good belief.

622. The best of manners is what keeps you away from the prohibited.

623. The best of nobility is shyness, and its fruit is chastity.

624. The best of manners is what takes you to do the generous things.

625. No dignity is higher than piety.

626. The best of saying is what to be proved by the good deeds.

627. The closest of all intentions to success are those accompanied with goodness.

628. Prayers are the offerings of every pious one.

629. The best of honour, is to stop hurting and to give.

630. The most successful of all the matters is what was surrounded by silence.

631. The happiest of people with goodness, are those who do it.

632. The best of characters are those of: generosity, chastity, and being calm.

633. The best of what people keep for themselves, the good conscious.

634. The bravest of people is he who wins over ignorance by kindness.

635. The best of garments is that of faith, and the best of what is kept is piety.

636. The happiest of all people is he who leaves a mortal lust for an immortal one.

637. The most noble of manners is generosity, and the most beneficial one is to be just.

638. The most faithful of people is he whose faith is not corrupted with lust.

639. The best of deeds, is to stop doing the ugly things.

640. The closest one to Allah is the one who has the best faith.

641. The thing that is most helpful for the fixation of the soul is, satisfaction.

642. The one who holds upon his honour the most, is the most generous.

643. The best of generosity is what comes out in time of misery.

644. The best of forgiveness is what is done with the ability (to punish).

645. The strongest of people is he who was strong upon his wrath by his kindness.

646. The most noble of people is he who made himself humble.

647. The one who knows Allah better, shall fear Him the most.

648. The best of generosity is to give the rights to their owners.

649. The purest of gains is the one who comes from Halal. [Halal means what is allowed by Allah, and opposite is Haram].

650. The best giving is what occurs before the humility of asking.

651. The best of manners is to give without asking (for something in return).

652. The origin of faith is to avoid the lusts.

653. The best of obedience is to ignore the lusts.

654. The one who knows Allah the best, is the one who is satisfied with His destiny the most.

655. The one who knows himself the best, is the one who fears his God the most.

656. The happiest one is the one who races to do the good deeds.

657. The best of manners is what you have started over yourself.

658. The best of shyness is when you are shy of yourself.

659. The best weapon is patience at the time of an adversity.

660. The most wise one is the one who escaped from the ignorant ones.

661. The happiest of all people is the one who lived along with the most generous people.

662. The greatest people in happiness are those who are most pious.

663. The origin of asceticism is the belief and its fruit is happiness.

664. The origin of determination is firmness and its fruit is winning.

665. The most firm of people is he who underestimates the matter of life.

666. The best of people is he who struggles against his lusts.

667. The origin of faith is to surrender to Allah for good.

668. The origin of satisfaction is to have a good trust in Allah.

669. The origin of patience is the good belief in Allah.

670. The origin of the strength of the heart is to depend on Allah.

671. The strongest of people is he who wins over his lust.

672. The most wise of all of the people is he who avoids every low deed.

673. The most satisfied of all people is he whose manners are all accepted.

674. The one who has the right mostly to be remembered by you, is he who never forgets you.

675. The one who has the right mostly to be thanked by you, is he who never minds increasing for you (in favours).

676. The one who has the right mostly to receive your kindness, is he who never stops being kind to you.

677. The one who has the right mostly to be rescued, is the one asking for forgiveness.

678. The best of giving is what to be given before asking for it.

679. The most honoured of all favours is what has been done to the people who deserve it.

680. The one who is the most able one to achieve the right things is the one who doesn't get angry.

681. The most blessed of all favours: satisfaction and a healthy body.

682. The best way to thank (Allah) for favours, is to do a favour with them.

683. The strongest of people is he who was strong upon himself.

684. The most noble of people is he who made himself humble.

685. The best of worshipping is to have a clean abdomen and honour.

686. The best of giving is to leave mentioning the favour's giving.

687. The best of piety is to have the good thought (about Allah).

688. The best of saying is what the deeds prove right.

689. The best of keepings is the good deeds.

690. The best medicine is to let go of wishing.

691. The best of truthfulness is to fulfil the promises.

692. The best of generosity is to give of what is available.

693. The best of sincerity is to do the promises.

694. The best of courage is to have passion.

695. The best of piety is to hide piety.

696. The most truthful of sayings is what coincides with the truth.

697. The one who has the most balanced of manners is the one who judges mostly with the right thing.

698. The most ornamented characters are those of kindness and chastity.

699. The best thing an able man can do is to forgive. [Able man here means the one who has the power or the authority to punish].

700. The best garment of faith is shyness.

701. The most useful of sermons is what makes an avoidance (from sins).

702. The best of things is piety.

703. The best honour is to give the goodness.

704. The best of faith is to have a good belief.

705. The best of people is the generous with belief.

706. The happiest of people is the wise and faithful.

707. The best of people is the one who is beneficial for the people.

708. The most wise of people is the one who pardons people.

709. The best of manners is the good courage.

710. The most noble of good manners is the good brotherhood.

711. The best of generosity is to complete the giving.

712. The best of noble manners is the high determination.

713. The strongest way, the good manners.

714. The most striking arrow is the prayer of the wronged one.

715. The best of justice is to be victorious to the wronged one.

716. The best of patience is at the time of the bitter adversity.

717. The most beneficial of treasures is the love of hearts.

718. The best of generosity is to forgive with the ability (to harm).

719. The best of obedience is to let go of lusts.

720. The highest rank in generosity is altruism.

721. The greatest owning is the owning of the self.

722. The best living is with satisfaction (for one has already).

723. The highest determination is the closest to generosity.

724. The most abundant of all of the favours is the health of the body.

725. The best favour is the rescue of the needy.

726. The best of works is what was done for the sake of Allah.

727. The best of the good deeds is what was done to people who deserve it.

728. The best of the good deeds is what was done to the good people.

729. The most fortified fort of religion is piety.

730. The most honourable lineage is the one of good manners.

731. The best of deeds is what coincides with the laws (of religions).

732. The best weapon is the good deeds.

733. The best of jihad (struggle) is what was done toward the self.

734. The best of good manners, generosity.

735. The most honourable of deeds is obedience (of Allah).

736. The best of living is to have satisfaction.

737. The best way is wisdom.

738. The best of generosity is altruism.

739. The best of faith is sincerity.

740. The best of nobility is the good manners.

741. The greatest of nobility is humility.

742. The bravest of all is the most generous.

743. The best of patience is to push oneself to be patient.

744. The best garment is piety.

745. The best shield is asceticism.

746. The thing that one should take pride in the most is the guidance.

747. Hajj (pilgrimage) is the jihad of the weak one.

748. The best of generosity is altruism.

749. The best of begging is to ask for forgiveness.

750. The most beautiful of gifts is to be just.

751. The best worshipping is to be pious.

752. The best of the faith is to do the good.

753. The best of happiness is the straightness of faith.

754. The best of religion, the belief.

755. The biggest of good deeds is passion.

756. The biggest if lineage is the good manners.

757. The best of saying is the right decision.

758. The most wise of you is the one who obeys (Allah) more.

759. The most merciful of you is the most pious of you.

760. The one who lives the most of you is the most kind of you.

761. The richest of you is the one who has the most satisfaction.

762. The most successful of you is the most truthful.

763. The smartest of you is the most pious of you.

764. The best thing is the good manners.

765. The most holy of things is truth.

766. The best of things is passion.

767. Mention Allah as much as you can for it is the best mention.

768. Own yourselves by struggling against it always.

769. Be together and avoid separation.

770. Reveal the fortune with charity giving.

771. Obey Allah according to what His messengers ordered you to do.

772. Work if you knew.

773. Be sincere if you worked.

774. Be easy and be humble in front of Allah and He shall raise you up.

775. Be satisfied with what you got and you shall have your enough.

776. Be satisfied about the fortune given to you and you shall have your enough.

777. Be satisfied for what is destined for you and you shall be a believer.

778. Be generous to your own self as long it (the self) helps you to obey Allah.

779. Be busy with giving thanks to the favour instead of singing about it.

780. Walk with your illness as long it allows you to do so.

781. Be in no need for whoever you want and be the same as him.

782. Be good to whoever you want and be his prince.

783. Make your work as your companion and your hope as your enemy.

784. Be just and the power shall last for you.

785. Keep your abdomen and your honour away from the prohibited.

786. Help your brother to guide him.

787. Control your wrath and your kindness shall increase.

788. Give this life away and the mercy shall be revealed upon you.

789. Always give thanks and the favour shall last for you.

790. Be good to the one who does badness to you and you shall own him.

791. Win over the lust and the wisdom will be complete for you.

792. Be good and others shall be good toward you.

793. Be generous to the ones you love and keep your promises.

794. Do your best and hold your bad.

795. Do against the ignorant and you shall be safe.

796. Obey the wise one and you shall gain.

797. Believe and be safe.

798. Give thanks and you shall be given more.

799. Be sincere and you shall gain.

800. Be a forgiver and you shall conquer.

801. Be generous and you shall be honoured.

802. Be patient and you shall reach.

803. Consider and you shall be convinced. [Consideration meant here is as to take the wisdom from examples and stories in life].

804. Be just and you shall own.

805. Be true and you shall succeed.

806. The good manners are the best of lineage and the most honourable of ways.

807. He whose brain wins over his lust shall be successful.

808. He who accepts the advice is safe from defaming.

809. Be satisfied and you shall relax.

810. Be kind and you shall be respected.

811. Learn the lessons and you shall stop doing evil.

812. Repent and you shall be given.

813. Do good and you shall enslave.

814. Obey and you shall gain.

815. Ask and you shall know.

816. Charity giving pushes away the adversity and the evil.

817. Praying is a fort against the attacks of Satan.

818. Confessing is the ally of the criminal.

819. Altruism is a mark for the faithful and a character of the good ones.

820. The wise one is the one who beholds his lust by his mind.

821. The perfect one, is he whose seriousness took over his pleasantry.

822. Fulfilling the promise is a sign of glory.

823. Generosity and shyness are the best of manners.

824. The person is by his smartness and not by his shape.

825. Piety is to stop at the steps of doubt.

826. The believer is he who protects his faith by his life.

827. The generous one is he who protects his honour with his fortune.

828. Obeying and doing goodness are the gainful trades.

829. Nobility is to be generous and fulfil the promises.

830. Charities reveal the mercy.

831. Chastity weakens the desire of lust.

832. The just one has many friends and loved ones.

833. The true believer is he who amongst all people fears the most for himself. [Fearing for himself comes in the meaning of fearing for the afterlife and not in the way of being a coward of course].

834. The generous one banished the shame and be generous to the neighbour.

835. To recommend the goodness is the best deed of creatures.

836. The wise one is he who protects his tongue against slander.

837. Completing the favour is better than its beginning.

838. Consulting is a relief for you and an exhaustion for others.

839. The faithful is a living, rich, a believer and a pious.

840. The faithful is a helper when he is asked, and a light one when he asks.

841. The satisfied one is a survivor from the beasts of greediness.

842. Avoiding the sins, that is the worshipping of the repentant ones.

843. Being generous for the sake of Allah, that is the worshipping of the close ones (to Allah).

844. Believing is the pillar of Islam and the pillar of faith.

845. The believer has the chastity when he is rich and giving up for this life.

846. Piety is the fruit of faith and a sign of believing.

847. The pious one is he whose soul got cleaned and his characters got honoured.

848. Justice is the head of faith and the collector of the good deeds.

849. Being patient for the adversity shall make the rewards abundant (later on).

850. Manners and religion are the results of the (good) mind.

851. The generous one is he who rewards the bad attitude with the good one.

852. The favour giver is he whose favours reach most of the people.

853. Bravery is a victory in advance and a virtue that is apparent.

854. The firm one is he who takes care of his time.

855. Sincerity leads to truthfulness.

856. Patience is the first thing needed for believing.

857. Truthfulness is the strongest pillar of believing.

858. Gaining the rewards of good deeds is the best of rewards.

859. The happy one is he who makes it easy for what he lost.

860. The generous one is he who gives from what is available.

861. Starting forgiveness is a character of the generous ones.

862. The generous soul is not affected by the adversities.

863. Being satisfied for what Allah had destined shall make the great adversities small.

864. Giving thanks is taken from those of favours.

865. Giving a favour is a treasure, so check out with whom you shall keep it.

866. Being satisfied with what is enough leads to chastity.

867. Giving charity in secret, that is the best of good deeds.

868. Charity prevents the bad deaths.

869. Consulting brings to you the correctness of others.

870. Being humble is the catch of nobility.

871. The faithful avoids the play and familiar with seriousness.

872. The satisfied one is a rich one though he might be hungry and naked.

873. The believer is just to those who are not just to himself.

874. Isolation is the best character of the smart people.

875. The mention (of Allah) is the guidance of the minds and the sight of the souls.

876. Obeying Allah is the strongest reason.

877. Work is all nothing, unless it was done with sincerity.

878. Being regretful about the sin avoids doing it again.

879. Thinking of evil as being ugly, that is a reason to avoid it.

880. Thinking about goodness, leads to doing it.

881. Shyness is the ornament of the girl.

882. Shyness protects against doing the ugly things.

883. The firm one is he who drops down the formality.

884. The beautiful deed foretells the high determination.

889. To stop asking for what is in the hands of the people, that is chastity and a high determination. [The wrong numbering is exactly found in the book, ignore it].

890. The wise one is he whose sayings coincide with his deeds.

891. The generous one is he whose giving precedes his asking.

892. To think good about someone is a character of the wise people.

893. The believer is an easy going with good manners.

894. The mention (of Allah) is the opener of the eyes' sights and the light of the interiors (of souls).

895. To be addicted to the truth, that is the best supply.

896. The brothers in faith are the ever lasting supply.

897. Checking the saying prevents the obstacles and mistakes.

898. Repentance cleans the hearts and washes the sins.

899. Sermons are the shapers of souls and the relief of the hearts.

900. To bear the low act that is one of the characters of the generous manners.

901. To give thanks, that is the ornament of the easy times and the fort of the favours.

902. The belief is patience in the time of adversity and thanks giving in the easy times.

903. The fighters on the way of Allah, the sky's gates are open for them.

904. The jihad (struggle) is the pillar of faith and the path of the happy ones.

905. To be passionate toward people, that is the head of wisdom.

906. To be good to the doer of badness, that is the best of giving.

907. Faith cannot be fixed except by mind.

908. Shyness is the completeness of generosity and the best of characters.

909. Kindness is a jewel of workings and the supply for peace.

910. Peace is the supply for safety and the sign of straightness.

911. To be patient over the bitter events shall leads to hitting the opportunity.

912. Piety is the most trustful fort and the most reliable charm.

913. Favours are the most growing plants.

914. Cooperating to achieve the truth is a charge and a way of faith.

915. The mind is a raise to the higher levels.

916. Generosity is to prefer honour over money.

917. Hoping for the mercy of Allah is more successful.

918. Working for the obedience of Allah is more beneficial.

919. Working with fixing the soul is more beneficial.

920. Depending on the destiny gives more relief.

921. Giving life away that is the great relief.

922. The brother of glory is he who obeys.

923. The brother of richness is he who covers himself with satisfaction.

924. Taking care (of people) is the most thankful of characters.

925. Giving condolences is the best of deeds.

926. Taking care when saying avoids the mistakes.

927. being patient when doing avoids the dangers.

928. The deeds in this life are the trade of the after-life.

929. Days will explain the hidden interiors.

930. The scholar is he who never gets fed up from learning.

931. The kind one is he who is never tired of being kind.

932. Being sincere about the work is from the might of the belief and the sincerity of the intention.

933. Giving thanks is the translator of the intention and the tongue of the interior.

934. Giving advice is a character of the generous ones.

935. Courage induces the generous manners.

936. Generosity is to bear the enemies.

937. Religion avoids the prohibited (acts).

938. The rich one is he who preferred the satisfaction (with what he has).

939. The happy one is he who was sincere about his obedience.

940. Wisdom in the foreign places makes you closer (to Allah).

941. The patient one got the opportunity or almost had.

942. The believer is a repentant and always asking for forgiveness.

943. The happy one is he whose belief is strong.

944. The wise one is he who takes the lessons from the (experience) of others.

945. The sign of the eloquence, an understanding heart and a saying tongue.

946. The good manners are the result of the (good) mind.

947. Wisdom is a guidance for him who works with it.

948. The mind is an ornament for him who had been given it.

949. The glorified one is he who takes glory in obedience.

950. The rich one is he who takes richness from satisfaction.

951. The good intention brings the rewards.

952. The firm one is he who stops harming others.

953. The wise one is he who gives.

954. The generous one is he who does the good.

955. The beginning of worshipping is to wait for the relief with patience.

956. Religion is a tree, its roots is made of surrender (to Allah) and being satisfied.

957. The mind is a tree and its fruit are generosity and shyness.

958. Truthfulness is the most honourable character of the believer.

959. Patience is the best soldier for the faithful.

960. Firmness and virtue are found in patience.

961. Patience is the supply to face the life.

962. The truthful one is on the edge of survival and dignity.

963. The believer is taken away from being astray (from the straight path) and debate.

964. Obedience turns down the wrath of God.

965. The wise man looks by the eyes of his heart and his mind.

966. The wise one depends on his work.

967. The wise man is he who knows his level.

968. The mind is a new garment that never gets old.

969. The signs of happiness is to be sincere about the work.

970. The patient one is right even though he might be doomed.

971. The generous one give thanks for the little.

972. The one consulting others is on the edge of success.

973. To regret for the sin, that is a repentance.

974. The one consulting others is fortified from falling down.

975. The one with experience is more wise than a physician.

976. The strong one is he who controls his lust.

977. The wise man is he who kills his lust.

978. The interior beauty is the good intention.

979. The wise one is he whom experiences taught him the lessons.

980. Correctness is a branch from patience.

981. Generosity is title of courage and nobility.

982. Kindness is a light with wisdom in its core.

983. The trust is a virtue for he who does it. [Trust as in deposit, "does it" means deliver it].

984. The sermons are a cure for him who works with them.

985. Chastity is the head of every good.

986. Surrender (to Allah) is to never accuse.

987. To think about the favours of Allah that is one of the best worshippings.

988. To hide poverty and sickness that is courage.

989. The helper who helps to do the obedience is the best of companions.

990. To show richness is a sign of giving thanks.

991. Giving favours is a supply and the generous one is he who has it.

992. Piety is a charm for who works with it.

993. Sincerity is a winning for who takes care of it.

994. The wise man is alive though he is dead.

995. Satisfaction (with what one has) leads to dignity.

996. Happiness is what leads to winning.

997. Learning the lessons leads to guidance.

998. Being pious leads to asceticism.

999. Truth saves you even though you might be scared of it.

1000. Truth is the fix for everything.

1001. The wise one is he who knows what he wants.

1002. The one controlling his wrath is he who kills his grudges.

1003. The kind one is he who bears his brothers.

1004. Faith is the base of piety.

1005. Satisfaction (about what one has) is the head of richness.

1006. Glory is to reach victory.

1007. Generosity is to have the good patience.

1008. Forgiveness is the best of victory.

1009. Obedience is to exalt the leadership.

1010. Leadership (imam-ship) is the system of the nation.

1011. Forgiveness brings glory.

1012. Generosity gains thanks giving.

1013. Being just makes love last longer.

1014. Paradise is the end of the winner.

1015. Obedience reveals the rewards.

1016. The confessor with his sins is a repentant.

1017. Charity is the treasure of the able.

1018. Doing good enslaves the human being.

1019. Truthfulness is the completeness of nobility.

1020. Humility is the ladder of honour.

1021. Health is the best of favours (of Allah).

1022. Shyness is the completeness of generosity.

1023. Piety is the fort of the believer.

1024. Hope is an amusing companion.

1025. Intention is the base of the work.

1026. Learning the lessons leads to guidance.

1027. Experiments are a useful science.

1028. Shyness is an acceptable manner.

1029. Mind is the component of science.

1030. Ignorance is opposite to firmness.

1031. Wisdom is the killer of ignorance.

1032. Paradise is the best goal.

1033. Wisdom is the most honourable guidance.

1034. Truth is the best story.

1035. Consulting is the core of guidance.

1036. Manners is the completeness of the man.

1037. Manners are the picture of the mind.

1038. Piety is a character of the scholars.

1039. Favours giving is the supply of eternity.

1040. The generous one is he who begins with his giving.

1041. Being just is the best of characters.

1042. Passion is the brother of the faithful.

1043. The deed is the companion of the believer.

1044. Health is the most blessed favour.

1045. Giving is the best of generosity.

1046. Being just is the best of generosity.

1047. Courage is to avoid the low deeds.

1048. Generosity is to be patient with wickedness.

ADAGES OF IMAM ALI (PUH) IN SOCIAL RELATIONS

1. The most devilish of brothers for whom formality must be set.

2. If a believer respected his brother (in a formal way) then he is separated from him.

3. Every new comer has a dilemma, thus make it easy for him with speech.

4. Every person entering (a new place) is surprised, thus start with saying peace (greeting).

5. Do not be hard on your brother for a doubt, and do not leave him after a blame.

6. The envy of the friend is a result of the sick affection.

7. Blame your brother by doing him good, and return his evil by doing favours for him.

8. No goodness exists in someone who leaves his brother for no crime.

9. No good is there in a miser friend.

10. No friendship for a friend would last with betrayal.

11. He would not be happy who makes troubles for his brothers.

12. Betrayal and brotherhood do not come together.

13. No friendship exists for one who gets bored easily.

14. The friendship of the well-mannered is the sweetest of all.

15. With justice, the brotherhood lasts.

16. The friendship is not clear unless with a well-mannered one.

17. Brotherhood is kept with giving condolences.

18. One of the greatest stupidities is to be a friend for the ill-mannered people.

19. The truthful friend is a gift.

20. He who has little determination, shall envy the friend for the favour.

21. He who has a low determination, do not be his companion.

22. He who cannot bear the mistakes of a friend, shall die lonely.

23. He who debates with his brothers shall have less friends.

24. He who has ill manners shall be left by his freinds.

25. He who digs a pit for his brother, Allah shall make him fall in it.

26. He who has no friends, has no supply.

27. He who has no brothers, has no family.

29. He who does not bear brotherhood, has no good in himself. [Wrong numbering in the book itself, ignore it].

30. If the friendship goes a long way, that is a sign of the good affection.

31. He who does not care about you, he is your enemy.

32. He who cares about you, he is your friend.

33. Friendship is enough as a test.

35. The good friendship is the goal of friends. [Wrong numbering in the book itself, ignore it].

34. The friend of the ignorant person is troubled and tired. [Wrong numbering in the book itself, ignore it].

36. The friend of the stupid is in tiresome time.

37. The friend of the stupid is exposed to damage.

38. Your friend is he who prohibits you, and your enemy is he who seduces you.

39. The condition for the friendship, is to have less objections.

40. May there be a brother for you that was not born by your mother.

41. The most devilish of your brothers is he who makes you satisfied by doing the ill deeds.

42. The good company makes love lasts.

43. The most devilish person you might company is the ignorant.

44. The good friendship increases the love in the hearts.

45. The most devilish of your brothers is he for whom you take formalities.

46. Ask about the companion before the road.

47. The most devilish of friends is he who flips back at you rapidly.

48. Forget about the bad things in the brothers and you shall make their affection last.

49. The most devilish of the friends is he who doubts a lot.

50. Ask about the neighbour before the house.

51. Damned is the bad neighbour.

52. By agreeing in good manners, the company shall last.

53. By living together in goodness, the affection shall last.

54. By being brothers unto (for the sake of) Allah, the brotherhood shall bear the fruit.

55. By living together in goodness, the companions shall be feeling good.

56. By being a good friend, the friends will be abundant.

57. By passion the friendship will last.

58. If the betrayal of the friend shows up, it would be easy to desert him.

59. The one who has the best gift is the one who starts the affection.

60. The priority for your affection goes to who does not desert you.

61. The best supply, the trustworthy of brothers.

62. The best of favours is to give condolences to the brothers.

63. Obey your brother even though he might disobey you, and tighten the relation with him though he might desert you.

65. The friend is the best supply and the most pious affection. [Wrong numbering in the book itself, ignore it].

66. Brothers are an ornament in the easy times and a supply in the time of adversity.

ADAGES OF IMAM ALI (PUH) IN MANNERS OF SPEECH AND SILENCE

1. Do not speak to the people about everything you hear, this is enough as a stupidity.

2. Do not use the bad words even though answering is hard for you.

3. No goodness lies in silence with wisdom, as there is no goodness in saying with ignorance.

4. Speak and you shall be known, for the person is hidden under his tongue.

5. Do not say what you do not know, but do not say everything you know.

6. If the mind is complete, speaking would be much lesser.

7. The tongue is a lion, if set free it would kill.

8. The heart of the stupid is in his mouth, and the tongue of the wise man is in his heart.

9. The tongue of the wise man is behind his heart, and the heart of the stupid is behind his tongue.

10. Being mute is better than lying.

11. Speech has beasts for it.

12. Blabbering too much shall make the guest bored and the boss dishonoured.

13. Muting is better than the ill speech.

14. Blabbering is a shame.

15. The tongue of everyone shall speaks for his mind.

16. The clue to the man's mind lies in the goodness of his speech.

17. The silly one shall not be straight except by the bitter speech.

18. Silence is a sign of kindness.

19. The tongue is the translator of the mind.

20. The clue to the mind of anyone lies in what goes on his tongue.

21. The best companion for kindness, silence.

22. No keeper is better than silence.

23. The wise one is he who holds his tongue back.

24. Do not lower someone until you make him speak.

25. It is part of the man's wisdom to not speak with everything he knows.

26. No keeper keeps more than silence does.

27. Who holds his tongue, is safe from regretting.

28. Who sets his tongue free, shows how silly he is.

29. No worshipping is like being silent.

30. Who gives bad talk in abundant, shall be blamed a lot.

31. Do not speak with what you are afraid to be not believed.

32. Who has a truthful speech, his clue shall be stronger.

33. Do not accompany who has no mind.

34. Who has the good speech, success lies in front of him.

35. Who has the bad speech, his luck shall be bad.

36. Who speaks a lot, shall be mistaken a lot.

37. Who answers rapidly, shall not know the right thing.

38. Who speaks a lot, people shall be bored with him.

39. Who has the sweet tongue shall have brothers in abundant.

40. For every level there is a speech.

41. Who speaks a lot shall be mistaken.

42. Who speaks in easy words shall be loved.

43. Who speaks a lot, his mistakes are abundant.

44. The truthful tongue for a man is more useful than money.

45. Who speaks a lot shall fall down a lot.

46. The speech of the man is the balance of his mind.

47. Who checks his speech shall be mistaken a little.

48. Who becomes silent is safe from being blamed.

49. Who speaks a lot is not safe from falling.

50. How many a blood that was shed by a mouth.

51. How many a word that took away a favour.

52. Who straightens his tongue, balanced his brain.

53. Straighten your tongue and you shall be safe.

54. Who speaks a little, his sins are less.

55. He is a winner, the silent pious one.

56. Who makes his tongue his own commander, killed himself.

57. The virtue of the man is known from his saying.

59. Who imprisons his tongue, is safe from regretting. [Wrong numbering in the book itself, ignore it].

60. The cover of bad things is silence.

61. Blessedness for him, who is silent except for the mention of Allah.

62. The silence of the ignorant is his veil.

63. The law of the means to say the ugly speech.

64. The mistake of the tongue would destroy the human being.

65. The reason for safety is silence.

66. May there be a word that stole away a favour.

68. May there be a blabbering that might bring evil. [Wrong numbering in the book itself, ignore it].

69. May there be a saying that is harder than a fight.

70. May there be a disturbance that was initiated by a saying.

71. May there be a saying whose answer is to be silent.

72. May there be a saying that silence is better than it.

73. May there be a tongue that destroys the human.

74. May there be a war that was started by a word.

75. The clue of the mind of the man is his saying.

76. The edge of the tongue is sharper than the edge of the sword.

77. The beautiful saying is a sign of the good mind.

78. May there be silence that is more eloquent than speech itself.

79. May there be a speech that penetrates more than arrows do.

80. To not answer the silly one, that is the best answer for him.

81. The adversity of the human lies in his tongue.

82. The speech of the man predicts his tongue's strength.

83. If you want to speak, say the truth.

84. If you talked, say the truth.

85. May the mercy of Allah be upon him who said good and gains, or went silent and been safe.

86. If the quantity of speeches was low, then the right things done are abundant.

87. The throw that hits the target the most, the right saying.

88. The silliest silly, is he who takes pride in the bad saying.

89. The most tiresome time for a wise man is when he speaks to a silly man.

90. The most low of wisdom is what stops on the tongue.

91. The best silence is toward the mistakes.

92. The worst of sayings is blabbering.

93. Be aware of blabbering, for whose talk is abundant, his sins are abundant as well.

94. Be aware of the tongue, for it is an arrow that might astray.

95. Avoid blabbering for the least thing it can bring is the blame.

96. Hold on the silence, for the least good thing it can do is give safety.

97. Hear and you will learn, and be silent and you will be safe.

98. Treasure your tongue, like you do with your gold and papers.

99. Lessen the talk and you are safe from the blame.

100. Be silent in your time and your matter will be glorified.

101. Hold on the silence and your thought will be enlightened.

102. Be silent and you shall be safe.

103. The wise man is he who tied his tongue except for the mention of Allah.

HIS ADAGES (PUH) ABOUT WISDOM AND WISE MEN, AND THE MIND AND THE MINDFUL MEN

1. Allah did not command the ignorant people to learn, until He commanded the people of wisdom to teach.

2. Wisdom is of two types: printed and heard, and the heard one is not useful if it is not printed.

3. If Allah wants to lower down a slave, He shall prohibit him from learning.

4. To stop learning, that is the excuse of those who call in sick.

5. Every container becomes narrower for what is put inside it, except of the container of science for it becomes wider and wider.

6. May there be a wise man who got killed by his ignorance, and his wisdom is with him but not beneficial to him.

7. Science saves.

8. Wisdom guides.

9. Wisdom is the ornament of the lineage.

10. The absence of the mind is between the desire and the lust.

11. The fruit of the thought is safety.

12. In the mind lies the benefit of the creations.

13. Wisdom is a generous heritage and a general gift.

14. The wise one is he who veils the sins with repentance.

15. Wisdom is the most glorified of goods.

16. Wisdom is the leader of kindness.

17. Wisdom is the killer of ignorance.

18. People are varied in their wisdom and their minds.

19. No one shall make low of wisdom and its people except of a stupid ignorant.

20. No sickness is more tiresome than having a low mind.

21. The little of wisdom enriches, and the little of ignorance dominates.

22. No wisdom for him who has no insight.

23. No mind for him who has no manners.

24. Wisdom is not purified without piety.

25. Wisdom is not taken with the relaxation of the body.

26. Wisdom is not beneficial without bless (from Allah).

27. Wisdom is the strongest base.

28. Wisdom is the best honour.

29. Wisdom is the most glorified cargo.

30. The respectfulness of the teacher is the ornament of wisdom.

31. The wise man is not seduced by the tricks of life.

32. He is not dead who revives a wisdom.

33. No understanding for him who does not keep on learning.

34. He is not wise who has a long hope.

35. No wisdom for him who exceeds his limit and his level.

36. How much are there who knows the wisdom and does not follow it.

37. No treasure is more useful than wisdom.

38. Nothing purifies the wisdom like doing it.

39. No glory is higher than wisdom.

40. Wisdom is the highest winning.

41. No guidance like thoughts.

42. No gift is best than having a mind.

43. Wise men are rulers over the people.

44. The mind is the spring of goodness.

45. The thought leads to guidance.

46. Wisdom is the best guide.

47. The gatherings of wisdom is a loot.

48. No mistake is harder than the mistake of the wise man.

49. The one who puts wisdom in some wrong place, then he wronged the wisdom.

50. He who knows, works.

51. No poverty is harder than ignorance.

52. One of the signs of the wisdom, is to work with justice.

53. Who took a seat over the mind, it shall carry him along.

54. No money is more beneficial than wisdom.

55. He who does not have a mind that ornaments him, then he is not a noble.

56. He who respects a wise man then respected his God.

57. He who has no wisdom, then do not ask him for something.

58. No companion like wisdom.

59. He who sits down with wisdom, ignorance shall stand up with him.

60. He who asks for guidance from wisdom shall be guided.

61. He who asks for help from the mind shall be successful.

62. He whose mind is complete, shall lower down his lusts.

63. He who loses his wisdom, had been slapped.

64. The seed of knowledge, is to study wisdom.

65. For everything there is a goal, and the goal of the person is his mind.

66. How many are there of humiliated people who got raised by their minds.

67. The gain of the mind is to stop harming (the others).

68. How many are there of noble ones who got humiliated by their ignorance.

69. The value of each person lies in his mind.

70. The gain of the wisdom is to let go of life.

71. The virtue of wisdom is to work with it.

72. The completeness of wisdom is work.

73. The completeness of the human is his mind.

74. Saying "I do not know" is half of the wisdom.

75. Wisdom is enough to raise someone.

76. The gain of the smart people is to study wisdom.

77. The veil of flaws is the mind.

78. The goal of the wisdom is to do the goodness.

79. Wisdom without work is like a tree without fruit.

80. The title of the virtue of the person, is his mind and his good manners.

81. The maximum of virtues, wisdom.

82. The minds of the virtuous ones are on the tips of their pens.

83. The highest of virtues, the mind.

84. The doubt of the wise one is more accurate than the certainty of the ignorant.

85. The highest of the wisdom is to fear Allah, the Exalted.

86. Wisdom without working is like a bow without a thread.

87. Two things that have no end: wisdom and the mind.

88. The zakat (almsgiving) of wisdom is to spread it.

89. Wisdom that is not useful, is like a medicine that does not cure.

90. Wisdom without working out, that is the claim of Allah over His slave.

91. The bad spot in wisdom is the pride.

92. The increment in the mind shall save.

93. The worst enemy of the mind, the pride.

94. The reason to fear (Allah), wisdom.

95. At the time of the natural speech, the minds of men are tested.

96. The most devilish adversity, the ignorance.

97. The level of the wisdom is the highest of all.

98. According to the level of the mind, religion shall be.

99. The most devilish of wisdom, what makes you lose your guidance.

100. Take care of the mind, for it is not compensated with money.

101. The best of hearts is the most conscious.

102. May there be a wise man who gains nothing.

103. The best of gifts is the mind.

104. The best of wisdom is what brings benefit.

105. The beauty of the mind is the beauty of the interiors and exteriors.

106. The good mind is the best leader.

107. The beauty of the wise man lies in working with his wisdom.

108. The heritage of wisdom lasts and saves.

109. The fruit of wisdom is to know Allah.

110. The fruit of the mind is to be straight.

111. To teach the wisdom, that is the zakat (almsgiving) of wisdom.

112. By wisdom, the level of kindness is achieved.

113. By the mind, the light of wisdom is extracted.

114. By the mind, goods are gained.

115. By learning, wisdom is gained.

116. By wisdom, life should be.

117. By wisdom, the bent shall be straightened.

118. By the minds, the ultimate of wisdoms are gained.

119. In the mind lies the repairing of every matter.

120. If Allah loved a slave of Him, He shall inspire him with wisdom.

121. The beast of smartness is deception.

122. The beast of the wise men is to love leadership.

123. The beast of wisdom is to leave working with it.

124. The beast of the public, an ill mannered wise man.

125. By thoughts, the hidden matters are illuminated.

126. The most helping thing to purify the wisdom is to teach it.

127. The most understanding of all the people, is the closest to Allah.

128. The most knowing of people is he whose doubt does not erase his certainty.

129. The most sinners of all people are the proud wise men.

130. The strongest of people is he who wins over his lust by his wisdom.

131. Mostly, the death of the minds comes under the lighting of greediness.

132. The clue to the rich mind is the good planning.

133. The greatest one with his wisdom is the one who fears Allah the most.

134. The most wise of people is him who obeys Allah the most.

135. The best of wisdom is what appears in the feelings and the limbs.

136. The best of wisdom what is accompanied by work.

137. The most wise of the people is the one who cares the most about people.

138. The origin of the mind is the thought and its fruit is safety.

139. The best of hearts is a heart that was filled with understanding.

140. The most noble of believers is the smartest.

141. The best of mind is to avoid entertainment.

142. The best of mind, that is manners.

143. The most honourable of honour, wisdom.

144. The beginning of the mind, affection.

145. The happiest of people is the wise.

146. The best of gifts is the mind.

147. The best of the mind is guidance.

148. The smartest of smartness is piety.

149. The most wise of people is he who obeys the wise men.

150. Gain wisdom to gain life.

151. Work with wisdom to be happy.

152. Ask for wisdom and you shall be guided.

153. Ask for guidance from the mind and oppose the lust and you shall succeed.

154. Obey wisdom and disobey the ignorance and you shall succeed.

155. The mind is a friend to be given thanks.

156. The smart one is he who veiled himself with shyness and had wisdom as a shield.

157. The smart one is he who owned the control of his lust.

158. The wise man is alive amongst the dead.

159. The ignorant is dead amongst the living.

160. Working with wisdom is a sign of the completeness of the favour.

161. The mind is the origin of wisdom and the tool to understand.

162. Wisdom is a ruler, and money is ruled.

163. Wisdom is a sign for the mind, and who knows is wise.

164. The wise men are strangers for the abundance of ignorant people.

165. Wisdom is a generous heritage and a general favour.

166. Wisdom is a great treasure that never ends.

167. The mind is a generous nobility that never wears out.

168. Wisdom without working is an adversity.

169. Wisdom is the lamp of the mind and the spring of virtues.

170. Wisdom leads to the truth.

171. Wisdom is the ornament of the rich ones and the richness of the poor ones.

ADAGES OF IMAM ALI (PUH) ABOUT THE HUMAN NATURE

1. People are enemies for what they do not know.

2. If a man has a famous character in him, then wait for its sisters.

3. If the ability was available, lust is lowered down.

4. In the turning of the situations, the cores of men are known.

5. Every type goes to a type like it.

6. Every person goes to a person like him.

7. The necessities of the situations humiliates the necks of men.

8. The most eloquent speech is what said by the tongue of the situation.

9. The most eloquent complaint is what to be said by the apparent adversity.

ADAGES OF IMAM ALI (PUH) ABOUT VICEROYS AND RULERS

1. Ruling shows the interior of men.

2. Authority is the gift of Allah on His land.

3. The tool of ruling, is the wide chest. [Wide chest means to have patience].

4. No ruling for him who is out of manners and runs after the play.

5. No domination for him who does not bear his brothers.

6. Justice is the virtue of the ruler.

7. Justice is he ornament of the leadership.

8. No injustice like the injustice of the ruler.

9. The viceroys of injustice are the most devilish of this nation.

10. The bad ministers are the helpers of the unjust ones and the brothers of the sinners.

11. Politics of passion is a good one.

12. Nothing gained countries like justice.

13. The rule is not complete for him who does not allow.

14. Who wrongs a ruler, then he offered himself for humiliation.

15. Who seeks the rule, should be patient for the bitterness of politics.

16. Who rules with injustice, people shall wish for his death.

17. Who takes pride in his rule, shall make his stupidity apparent.

18. Who owned shall monopolize.

19. Who was unjust in his ownership, he shall speed up his doom.

20. Who fears your whip, shall wish for your death.

21. Who entrusts your goodness, shall have the pity on your rule.

22. It is but a few that the companions of the kings do last.

23. In injustice, lies the doom of the people.

24. Whose rule was unjust, his land shall be doomed.

25. In justice, the fixation of the people.

26. The fix of the people is justice.

27. The most devilish of kings is he who opposes justice.

28. The most devilish of viceroys, whom the innocent fears the most.

29. A mighty lion that eats too much, is better than a viceroy that is ignorant and unjust.

30. The most devilish of princes, whose lust was a prince over him.

31. The ornament of the king, justice.

32. The time of the just is the best of times.

33. The time of the unjust is the most devilish of times.

34. The head of politics is to use passion.

35. The best of politics, justice.

36. It is a right upon the king to train himself before his soldiers.

37. The love of rule, that is the head of adversities.

38. The good justice, that is the system of the creations.

39. The good politics, that is the straight path of the people.

40. The good politics, shall make ruling last.

41. The generosity of the viceroys with the money of the Muslims, that is unjust and evil.

42. The stability of lands is based on justice.

43. The crown of the king is his justice.

44. Your pride in ruling, is humility when isolated.

45. The worst of friends are the kings.

46. The worst of politics is injustice.

47. By justice, the blesses are multiplied.

48. By justice, the people are fixed.

49. If you are made a viceroy, then be just.

50. If the lower ones ruled, then the virtuous ones shall die.

51. When the means conquer, the generous shall be wronged.

52. If the time turned bad, at then, the mean ones shall rule.

53. If the ruler made you closer, then glorify him more. [It is apparent that this phrase concerns the just ruler, or it is in the way of avoiding the harm of the ruler].

54. The beast of the kings is the bad reputation.

55. The beast of the leaders, the bad politics.

56. The beast of ruling, the pride.

57. The most dignified of princes, whose lust was not a prince over him.

58. The most dignified of kings is he who owned himself and spread justice.

59. The best of kings in manners is he who owns the people with his justice.

60. The best of kings whose soul was more chaste.

61. The most ugly thing (in life), the injustice of the viceroys.

ADAGES OF IMAM ALI (PUH) IN THE BAD HABITS AND AVOIDING THEM

1. Slander is the work of the unable.

2. Every time someone plays a joke, he spits some part of his brain.

3. Who enlarges the little problems, Allah shall send over him the big ones.

4. Who trades without knowledge, then he crashed with usury.

5. Who fights against the truth shall be doomed.

6. Who wants to keep his honour, then let him let go of disputes.

7. The biggest shame is to say about something it is a shameful thing, and you have something like it.

8. Avoid what Allah had prohibited when you are alone, for the Witness is the Ruler (Himself).

9. A jealous man never commits adultery. [Jealousy has different levels, and the level meant here is the fear of man upon his honour, and not the doubt of man about his wife].

10. The greedy is tightened by humility.

11. Dispute destroys the opinion.

12. The wonder of someone about himself, that is one of the jealousies of his mind.

13. Wondering avoids increments.

14. A man that does not know his level is doomed.

15. Greed is an eternal enslavement.

16. Who quitted saying "I do not know" his doom approached.

17. Who has the long hope, does the bad deeds.

18. Wronging (people) overtakes the favours.

19. Insisting (on bad things) brings the hell.

20. The free man is a slave as long he is greedy.

21. No rest for the envious.

22. Who obeys laziness shall squander the rights.

23. Injustice is enough to overtake the favours.

24. Misery (keeping money) is attached to tiresome times.

25. It is of misery to have the bad intentions.

26. Let go of playing jokes, for it is the seed of hate.

27. Wronging is a crime that shall not be forgotten.

28. The few of hypocrisy is infidelity.

29. No badness uglier than being proud of the good deeds.

30. The lasting ignorance blinds the insight.

31. The few of doubt disturbs the certainty.

32. No humility is greater than greed.

33. Whose hope was long, his deeds shall be bad.

34. The lasting injustice overtakes the favours and brings the adversities.

35. No one has pride unless he is a humiliated and a lazy one.

36. Nothing as bad as being a miser.

37. Greed is a humility in attendance.

38. The little greed spoils the abundance of piety.

39. No cheater and no one with pride of his good deeds shall enter paradise.

40. Humility is in begging people.

41. No lust there is in a finite lust.

42. The ignorant is a slave to his lust.

43. The envious never gets well.

44. No adversity is greater than envy.

45. Hypocrisy is the brother of infidelity.

46. The greedy is never satisfied.

47. The listener to the slander is like the one who says it.

48. No ill manner like cruelty.

49. The traitor has no loyalty.

50. The fighter against truth is hated.

51. Whoever takes pride in his deeds, his thanks giving is dropped.

52. No lust there is for the one who does the good deed with pride.

53. With time being late, shall be the regret.

54. Pride is the eye of the stupidity.

55. One of the greatest miseries, the cruelty.

56. No faith for a cheater.

57. Who likes his deeds, his rewards are dropped.

58. Squandering money is the title of poverty.

59. With hurry, mistakes are abundant.

60. No ignorance is greater than pride.

61. Who asks for glory without a right, then shall be humiliated.

62. Slandering is the sign of hypocrisy.

63. No manner is uglier than pride.

64. Who is proud of doing a favour, did not do it completely.

65. Who is not satisfied about his destiny, infidelity entered his religion (faith).

66. Disputing a lot is tearing.

67. How miserable is the living of the envious.

68. Who did not believe in the reward (good or bad), then his faith got interrupted with doubt.

69. Blabbering too much brings the shame.

70. Nothing is a liar like the hope.

71. The infidel is an infidel because he does not know.

72. Excusing too much, that is the sign of a miser.

73. So much greed, that is the title of the lessened piety.

74. No faith for whose repentance is always delayed.

75. No one is proud unless he is a low one.

76. Ignorance is enough to put someone down.

77. Who enlightens the fire of disturbance, shall be a fuel for it.

78. Wishing too much is a sign of the bad mind.

79. No health there is with a greedy.

80. How ugly is misery (with money) in abundance.

81. Who is proud of his good deeds, then as if he did not do any.

82. Who plants hatred shall gain the adversities.

83. Too much hatred is tiresome for the hearts.

84. Pride is enough to be a corruptor.

85. No favour for the one who takes pride with his good deeds.

86. The worst of injustice, is to be unjust toward the generous (nobles) ones.

87. No victory with injustice.

88. The worst of treachery, to be treacherous about deposits.

89. Squandering is enough to be an ill manner.

90. Being full (of stomach) makes diseases abundant.

91. No sickness is more severe than stupidity.

92. No character is worse than telling lies.

93. No one likes his opinion except of an ignorant.

94. The ugliest thing in treachery is to spread a secret.

95. From the mean ones, cruelty comes.

96. Nothing worsens religion like greed.

97. The ugliest thing in ill manners, the slander about the good people.

98. Silliness is enough to be a shame.

99. Nothing can be achieved with stupidity.

100. Religion is doomed by the desires.

101. Who does not give thanks for the favour, is forbidden from getting more.

102. No smartness with greed for food.

103. Because of dispute, people do not hit the target.

104. Pride is enough to be a humiliation.

105. No faith with the bad thought.

106. Who protects his secret from you then he accused you.

107. No shyness for a miser.

108. Who takes his own opinion, then he took the risk and seduced.

109. Greed is linked to humiliation.

110. Who wronged himself, then he shall more wrong to others.

111. No faith for him who has the bad thought.

112. Who is victorious to the unjust, shell be regretful.

113. In obeying the desire, lies all the errors.

114. Who wronged people, then Allah is his opponent.

115. No strangeness like misery (of money).

116. Who treats with injustice, shall be rewarded the same.

117. Who has no faith, has no rescue.

118. In obeying the self lies its own error.

119. No right in letting go of consulting.

120. Who paid evil for goodness shall be a loser.

121. The treachery of a man is a shame for him.

122. Who works with the not important shall miss the important.

123. No sickness like envy.

124. Who cares about the fortune of tomorrow shall never be successful.

125. In silliness and playing jokes too much lies the stupidity.

126. Chasing after the privacy of others, is one of the greatest shames.

127. No humiliation like begging.

128. Who took out the sword of treachery, then it shall be planted in his head.

129. The addict of lusts shall have many illnesses.

130. No enemy like the desire.

131. An honourable man is never unjust.

132. Who delivers to you a swear, then he swore at you.

133. Who exceeds his limits, shall be lowered by the people.

134. No favour with infidelity.

135. The gatherings of fun shall disturb the faith.

136. Misery (of money) brings the troubles.

137. Who is satisfied about himself, then so many shall be angry about him.

138. The pride of the low, is an invitation to lower him down.

139. Who does not fix himself, shall not fix the others.

140. No affection for an envious.

141. Who gets the full stomach, smartness shall be veiled from him.

142. Any two shall swear at each other, then the meanest of them shall win.

143. Who does not own his lust, then he does not own his mind.

144. Following after the flaws, is one of the ugliest shames and the most devilish of sins.

145. No faith for a traitor.

146. A chaste man never commits adultery.

147. Who gives you the news, spreads the news about you.

148. The poverty of the soul is the most devilish of poverty.

149. The corruption of religion, the greed.

150. Who does not grow his favour then he lost it.

151. No faith for a doubtful one.

152. The one using misery is a shameful and miserable one.

153. Who gives a favour and becomes proud of it, did not feel the satisfaction of it.

154. Desperation killed its owner.

155. Who gets owned by the greed then he is humiliated.

156. A little of greed spoils the faith.

157. No shyness for a liar.

158. He is doomed, who does not know his level.

159. Who enjoys doing the prohibitions of Allah, then He shall give him humiliation.

160. The dictator went wrong.

161. Who accuses himself then he is safe from the tricks of the devil.

162. Who rode over the sins shall be regretful.

163. No courage for a slanderer.

164. Who lies is doomed, and who claims is disappointed.

165. To hurry up the revenge, that is a character of the means.

166. A believer is never in doubt.

167. Who rode over his hopes, shall be troubled with his end.

168. Who was in hurry shall be humiliated.

169. Misery killed its rider.

170. Who is proud about himself, then his self shall drive him to the troubles.

171. The opinion of the one in hurry is rarely correct.

172. Who opposes the advices shall be doomed.

173. The black spot of generosity, squandering.

174. Who treats (others) with violence shall be regretful.

175. The reason to corrupt the belief, the greed.

176. Who was generous to himself, his self shall humiliate him.

177. The head of shames, the greed.

178. Who was ignorant to his self, then he doomed his self.

179. The reason for the corruption of the mind, the desires.

180. Who enters the entries of badness, shall be accused.

181. The result of hopes, the sorrow.

182. Who was satisfied about his own opinion then he is doomed.

183. The result of sins, the damage.

184. Who fights against the truth then shall lose.

185. The reason for disturbances, the envy.

186. The adversity is one, and if you are afraid, then they are two (adversities).

187. The result of hopes, the sorrow, and its fruit is the damage.

188. Who laughs a lot, then his respect is lessened.

189. The reason for the removal of the favours is the infidelity.

190. Who forgets Allah, He shall make him forget himself as well.

191. The obedience to misery is corruption to the belief.

192. The fruit of squandering is the blame.

193. Who has the bad thoughts, then his interior is bad as well.

194. The head of flaws, the envy.

195. Who jokes, is taken light.

196. The fruit of the late time, the regret.

197. Who liked himself shall be mocked at.

198. How hard is the sickness of stupidity.

199. Who mocked at something shall be troubled with it.

200. The head of ignorance, the injustice.

201. Who made himself great then shall be put down.

202. Obeying hope shall make the work worsen.

203. Who obeyed his self, he would kill it.

204. The head of the ill manners, the envy.

205. Who was in hurry shall face many obstacles.

206. How hard is the company of misery.

207. Who asks for guidance from someone was sent astray, then shall be sent astray.

208. Obeying desire corrupts the mind.

209. Who asks for help from a humiliated person shall be humiliated.

210. The fruit of hurrying, falling down.

211. Who cares less, shall face his doom.

212. Who does not notice shall have a hard time.

213. The fruit of liking (the self), the hatred.

214. Miserable is the character of slandering.

215. Who makes himself silly, shall be cursed.

216. The head of infidelity, treachery.

217. The fruit of greed, troublesome times.

218. Who offered his honour, shall be humiliated.

219. The fruit of the dispute, hatred.

220. The worst of all greed, the greed for food.

221. Who has a pride shall be humiliated.

222. Obeying women is the ultimate ignorance. [This is because the emotional side in a woman is greater than it would be in a man].

223. The head of ignorance, to be an enemy to the public.

224. The worst of all food, the Haram. [Haram means anything illegal or came by illegal ways].

225. Who pretends to be poor, shall be poor.

226. The fruit of the pride, the curse.

227. Who takes his opinion only, shall make a mistake.

228. The worst food ever, what was got by the money of an orphan.

229. Who had his enough with his mind shall be sent astray.

230. The head of all beasts, the love of lusts.

231. Who fight against the truth shall be dead.

232. The worst of necklaces, the necklace of sins.

233. Who wrongs (people), his life time shall be short.

234. Who got scared, his adversity shall be huge.

235. The injustice of a person shall make him fall down and kill him.

236. Who has no sincerity, has no faith.

237. The worst of habits, curiosity.

238. Whose reputation was bad, for his death people shall be glad.

239. He is sent astray, who was guided by something else other than the guidance of Allah.

240. Who planned in a bad way, his destruction would come right away.

241. The worst of all companions, the ignorant.

242. Who has the pride over people shall be humiliated.

243. The worst of friends is the envious.

244. Who rode over his desires shall fall down.

245. The injustice toward the weak, that is the evil of the injustice.

246. The worst of all speeches, the lie.

247. Who liked his own opinion then shall be sent astray.

248. The most devilish thing that one can occupy his leisure time with is, curiosity.

249. By injustice, the favours are taken out.

250. Who laughs a lot shall be put down.

251. By lying, the hypocrites ornament themselves.

252. Who plays a lot, shall be thought of as stupid.

253. The worst of deeds, the sin.

254. The injustice toward the surrendering person, that is the greatest crime.

255. The most devilish of people is he who thinks he is the best of them.

256. Who thinks himself to be safe from the trials of Allah then he is doomed.

257. The injustice toward the favours, that is the ugly pride.

258. The fruit of misery (of money), tiredness.

259. Who is glad for the corruption, shall feel bad for the after-life.

260. The fruit of arguing, the damage.

261. The worst of all supplies, doing the evil.

262. Whose play is much, his mind is lessened.

263. The obedience of the desire can be a killer.

264. The worst of injustice, the injustice toward the surrendering one.

265. Whose envy lasts long, then his grief shall be long.

266. The fruit of the inability, missing the chance.

267. To leave doing the sin, that is hard, and harder than that is to let go of paradise.

268. The worst of gains is the Haram.

269. Whose character is occupied by jest, his mind then is less.

270. By pride, the favour-giving is corrupted.

271. The winning of the mean shall be fatal.

272. The most devilish of people is, who people avoid him for his evil.

273. The worst companion for faith, the greed.

274. By injustice, the wrath is brought.

275. Being unjust toward the slaves (of Allah), that corrupts the after-life.

276. The most devilish of manners of the soul, the injustice.

277. The worst of men is he who sells his faith for the sake of another man's life.

278. The most devilish of opinions, is what opposes the law.

279. The increment in lust, puts down the courage.

280. The worst of lineage, the bad manners.

281. The most devilish of all deeds is what collapses the good deeds.

282. Your desire for someone that does not recognize you is humility.

283. The worst of works is to work on separating two people loving each other.

284. The ego is summed in being asleep in front of the enemy.

285. The worst necklace, is the necklace of debt.

286. The most devilish of people, is the one who wrongs the people.

287. Your desire in the impossible is an ignorance.

288. The worst of readiness, the dictatorship.

289. For the aggressor, there is a bad end.

290. When the intention is bad, the bless is removed up.

291. The worst supply for the after-life, that is aggression upon the slaves (of Allah).

292. Who laughs a lot, his heart shall die.

293. The goal of the infidel, the hell.

294. The worst habit, misery.

295. Who counts his favours, his generosity shall be destroyed.

296. The reason for hatred, arguing so much.

297. By being scared a lot, the adversity is enlarged.

298. Whose habits were bad, his family shall be tired of him.

299. When the reputation is bad, the interior becomes corrupted.

300. Who lies a lot, his truth shall not be believed.

301. May there be a cheater, that got killed by his cheating.

302. Delaying work, is a sign of laziness.

303. Who jokes a lot, his respect is lessened.

304. The fruit of doubts, bafflement.

305. Keeping on watching a flaw, that is shameful.

306. Whose manners are low, his flaws are abundant.

307. Lessening the sin, is greater than doing it.

308. Who fights against the one above him shall be a loser.

309. The rider of the sin shall be in hell.

310. Who accompanies misery, shall be not given the advices.

311. The pride of a person shall be put him down.

312. Who opposes the truth, Allah shall be his opponent.

313. The fruit of envy is the tiredness of life and the after-life.

314. The most devilish of people, who cheats upon the people.

315. The rider of injustice shall be reached by the loss.

316. The fruit of greed, the humiliation of this life and the after-life.

317. By pride, the favour-doing is neglected.

318. The most devilish of deeds, is what brings the sins.

319. The rider of arguments shall be exposed to the adversity.

320. The bad neighbour is the greatest hard time and the hardest adversity.

321. The fruit of hope, the corruption of the deed.

322. Who insisted on asking shall be banned.

323. Being satisfied about yourself is a sign for your bad mind.

324. Who insists has no planning.

325. An hour of humiliation does not fill to the dignity of the life time.

326. The rider of injustice, shall be flipped by his own boat.

327. A miser has no beloved one.

328. In misery lies the curse.

329. The rider of violence, it is hard for him to reach his goal.

330. The cutter of kinship relations has no relatives.

331. The most devilish of people, who helps against the wronged one.

332. The hearer of the slander is one of the slanderers.

333. Being scared bears no rewards.

334. The most devilish of children, the disobedient.

335. Riding the greed, cuts the necks of men.

336. The mean has no courage.

337. The habit of the evil ones, to oppose the good ones.

338. The habit of the evil ones, to harm the companions.

339. It is not of generosity to cut the kinship relations.

340. The most devilish of manners, lying and hypocrisy.

341. Riding the bad habits, that is the title of stupidity.

342. Squandering bears no honour.

343. The reason of corruption in piety, the greed.

344. Who asks for help from the weak, shows how weak he is.

345. May there be a deed that gets corrupted by the intention.

346. Who gets closer to the silly one, that shows how silly he is.

347. The beauty of evil, the greed.

348. Who sold his after-life for the sake of his life, then he lost both.

349. The reason of wickedness, being alone.

350. May there be a proud man that gives the heritage of corruption.

351. Who accompanies the evil ones shall not be safe.

352. The bad planning is the reason of destruction.

353. Avoid disappointing, deserting and cutting the kinship relations.

354. Whose worries are a lot, his body shall be sick.

355. May there be a cautious (a miser) who got killed by his own caution (misery).

356. Whose anxieties are a lot, his sadness is eternal.

357. An envious man has no friends.

358. Avoid treachery, for it is an avoidance of Islam.

359. Who lives for long time, his adversities are abundant.

360. The most devilish thing that would live in the heart, the grudge.

361. Avoid back-stabbing, for it is an avoidance to the Quran.

362. Who has no shyness, no goodness lies in him.

363. The bad manners are the troubles of living and the torture of the soul.

364. Neglecting the good deed, brings the prohibition.

365. The evil is summed in the company of the bad friend.

366. The bad manners are the most devilish of friends.

367. Who begs people so much, shall be humiliated.

368. The miser has no companion.

369. The slave of the lust is humiliated more than the slave of enslavement.

370. Who opposes the truth, shall be accompanied by weakness.

371. Lying is not a habit of the prophets.

372. The law of the mean ones, to deny the favour.

373. Who blames the men, then his enemies are a lot.

374. The proud one has no friends.

375. The shame of the defame, spoils the sweetness of the lust.

376. The bad intentions is a deep sickness.

377. Who lies a lot, his halo is lessened.

378. Cutting the kinship relations has bears no growth.

379. The weapon of meanness, the envy.

380. Whose lust is abundant, his courage is lessened.

381. Envy is not a character of the pious.

382. The slave of the misery, is eternal in his troublesome times.

383. To ask for paradise with working, that is stupidity.

384. Whose aggression lasts longer, his authority would be destroyed.

385. Flattery was not a manner of the prophets.

386. The one asking for goodness from the mean people shall be banned.

387. Who rides the speed, reaches the flaws.

388. By greed, the manners are corrupted.

389. If worshipping is lessened, sins are grown up.

390. By pride, hatred starts.

391. If the minds were lessened, then curiosity is grown up.

392. By laziness, missing the chance comes.

393. If doubts present themselves, the thoughts would go bad.

394. By misery, the troublesome time comes.

395. If the sins of the friend were so much, then happiness around him is lessened.

396. By desperation, doom is assured.

397. If the pious runs after people, then escape away from him.

398. According to the level of happiness, shall be the disturbance.

399. If the mean glorified you more, then humiliate him more.

400. According to the abundance of wrath, shall be the rashness.

401. The beast of faith, infidelity.

402. By avoiding the truth, error would be.

403. The beast of the belief, the doubt.

404. By doubting all the time, infidelity comes.

405. The beast of giving favours, neglecting them.

406. By being proud too much, corruption shall be.

407. If you did a good deed to a mean one, he shall trouble you with what you give him.

408. By avoiding the low deeds, you shall be safe from torture.

409. If the intention was bad, the adversity shall be revealed.

410. By greed, the necks of men shall be humiliated.

411. The beast of the honour, the pride.

412. The beast of kindness, humiliation.

413. The beast of economy, misery.

414. In evil lies rudeness.

415. The most unjust of people, who considers his injustice to be justice issued from his side.

416. In misery lies the tiredness.

417. The most destructive thing, the ever lasting error.

418. The evil that is punished for the fastest, the injustice.

419. The greatest of sins, a sin that was insisted upon by its doer.

420. The beginning of the desire (lust), disturbance, and its end is a trouble.

421. The weakest of enemies, is he who shows his enmity.

422. The ugliest of sins, cutting the kinship relations and disobedience (to parents).

423. The most regretful thing, the pass of chances.

424. What is harder than death, asking for something from people who are not capable of it.

425. The the most miserable one, who was a miser for greeting.

426. The most unjust of people, is he who was unjust to someone who was just to him.

427. The biggest shame, is to mock at something that you have in yourself.

428. The man troubled the most, is he who sells his religion for the life of someone else.

429. The ugliest of misery, to ban the money from the people deserving it.

430. He spoiled his religion who got naked of piety.

431. He got himself down who felt the greed in himself.

432. The beginning of lust, pleasure, and its end is to damage.

433. The beginning of fun, a play, and its end is to war.

434. The most hated creature for Allah is the doubtful (about his faith).

435. The affection that is the fastest to be over, the affection to the evil ones.

436. The worst injustice, if you banned the rights of Allah.

437. The most humiliated of people, is he who is not respectful to people.

438. The stupidest of people, is he who thinks he is the smartest of people.

439. The most unable of people, is he who is unable to pray (to Allah).

440. The one of people who has the longest hope, has the worst deeds.

441. The one of people who has abundance in hopes, remembers death a little.

442. The hardest of tasks, is to ask for what is in the hands of the mean ones.

443. The hardest thing is the unjust of the judges.

444. The ugliest excuse, is to spread the secret. (?)

445. The greatest of burden, is to not accept the excuse.

446. The ugliest thing an able man would do, is to revenge.

447. The greatest meanness, is to praise the cursed.

448. The meanest aggression, is at the time of ability (to do so).

449. The greatest burden, to make the evil ones pure.

450. The greatest adversity, the poverty of the soul.

451. The ugliest truthfulness, is the praise of a man to himself.

452. The greatest treachery, is the treachery of the nation.

453. The most awful cheating, is cheating on the imams (leaders).

454. The worst of truthfulness, the slander.

455. The greatest ignorance, is the ignorance of man toward himself.

456. The worst man in living is the envious.

457. Who exaggerated in enmity is a sinner.

458. The most humiliated of people is the doubtful.

459. The ugliest of manners is treachery.

460. The ugliest of manners, greed.

461. The ugliest of characters, the pride.

462. The most troubled of people is the ignorant.

463. The most harmful thing is the greed.

464. The most harmful thing is the stupidity.

465. The worst thing ever is the stupidity.

466. The most destructive thing is the desire.

467. The strangest estrangement, is to like oneself.

468. The ugliest of characters is telling lies.

469. The ugliest of giving, the squandering of money.

470. The greatest adversity, is the stop of hope.

471. The most troubled of you, is the most miserable of you.

472. The greatest of troubles, the ignorance.

473. The most lying thing, the hope.

474. The poorest of poverty is stupidity.

475. Be aware of injustice, for the unjust person will not even smell the scent of paradise.

476. Be aware of the addiction of satisfaction (of food), for it raises up the sicknesses and illnesses.

477. Be aware of showing wickedness, for it is one of the hardest sins.

478. Be aware of hurrying up, for it is accompanied by falling down.

479. Be aware of stupidity, for it is the blackness of the manners.

480. Be aware of being silly, for it makes the companions lonely.

481. Be aware of being greedy (for food), for it spoils the piety and gets you into hell.

482. Be aware of anger, for its beginning is madness and its end is regret.

483. Be aware of being in hurry, for it is the title of missing and regret.

484. Be aware of injustice, for who wrongs (people), his days are hated.

485. All be aware of hopes, for they are an assured doom.

486. All be aware of anger, for it is a burning fire.

487. All be aware of envy, for it lowers down the soul.

488. All be aware of ignorance, for it is the corruption of the sense.

489. All be aware of misery, for it is meanness and a curse.

490. All be aware of cowardice, for it is a shame and a lessening in character.

491. All be aware of being hurry, for it inherits the regret.

492. All be aware of squandering (the money), for it reveals the blame.

493. All be aware of greed (of food), for it is a deadly character.

494. All avoid the evil, for the most devilish of evil is the doer.

495. All avoid misery, because its companion is captivated in humiliation and tiresome times.

496. The desires are a worshipped god.

497. Ingratitude, spoils the favour and reveals the wrath.

498. The grudge is a character of the evil ones.

499. The pride is a character of the low ones.

500. Fun spoils the might of seriousness.

501. Wrath reveals the hidden grudges.

502. Being proud of the sins is worse than riding them (doing them).

503. The mean one is worn the shame and harm the free men.

504. The pride is a fatal character, and who grows with it shall be lessened.

505. The stone that was taken by force in a house, is a sign for its corruption.

506. Hunger is better than the humility of submission.

507. Joking is a separation followed by hatred.

508. The envious one is always a sick man, and the miser is always a humiliated man.

509. The miser is a poor man even if he owned the corners of the world.

510. Wrath kills its owner and exposes his flaws.

511. Being a miser gains the shame and gets you into the hell.

512. The bad manners is one of the two tortures.

513. The cheater has a sweet tongue and bitter heart.

514. The hypocrite's tongue gives a delight, and his heart gives the harm.

515. The hypocrite has a beautiful exterior, and a sick interior.

516. Wickedness and being wicked, are not of Islam.

517. Lying and treachery are not characters of the honourable ones.

518. Aggression kills the men and make their ends near.

519. The envious one is happy with evil and sad with happiness.

520. Sadness and fear shall not get back what passed away.

521. Being led by the lust, that is the sickest illness.

522. The hopes trick you, and with the facts they leave you.

523. The miser is humiliated amongst his close ones.

524. Misery humiliates its companion, and glorifies the one avoiding it.

525. The favour is disturbed by repeating the pride about it.

526. The ignorant is he who cheats with the advice.

527. The adversity in religion is one of the greatest adversities. [Adversity in religion means that someone is in doubt about his own belief].

528. Life is a dream and being seduced by it, that is a regret.

529. Slandering is an unforgettable sin.

530. Envy is a sickness with no condolences.

531. Hopes make the eyes of the insight blind.

532. Poverty makes the smart one clueless about his argument.

533. The tyrant with injustice shall fall down by his sins.

534. The sleepy rider is accused of lying by his own dreams. (?)

535. The miser is a prisoner of humility and his captivity is never released.

536. Praising makes a state of pride, and gets you closer to the high state.

537. Preferring the luxury, cuts out the reasons of benefit.

538. Addiction to satisfaction (of food) inherits the reasons of pains.

539. Hope corrupts the work, and squander the end.

540. Anger corrupts the mind and blinds the eyes from the right path.

541. Ignorance slides the feet and inherits the regret.

542. Anger is an enemy, thus do not give yourself to it.

543. Being in hurry before the ability reveals the regret.

544. To dare to face the ruler, that is the greatest doom.

545. Being satisfied without the kings, that is the best ownership.

546. Racing to help the untruthfulness is meanness and treachery.

547. Meanness is to love money more than men.

548. Poverty with debt, that is the greatest tiredness.

549. Cheating is a character of the mean.

550. Being stupid in the homeland that is estrangement.

551. One in hurry is mistaken or almost he is.

552. The hypocrite is harmful and doubtful.

553. The tricked one is he whose faith is corrupted.

554. The ignorant is he who gets tricked by his desires and ego.

555. The hated manners are a result of the ignorance.

556. Silence without a thought is muteness.

557. Thinking in something else other than wisdom is madness.

558. The miser argues about excuses.

559. Untruthfulness are falling on destiny.

561. Blabbering conquers love. [Wrong numbering in the book itself, ignore it].

562. Gathering (the clues) weakens the argument.

563. Blabbering is close to the adversities.

564. The mean is he who gets proud repeatedly.

565. Being miser with what is available, that is a bad thought about the Worshipped (Allah).

566. The liar is on the edge of pit and humility.

567. Faith is innocent of hypocrisy.

568. Doubt turns off the light of the heart.

569. The ignorant looks by his eyes and sight.

570. The ignorant depends on his hope.

571. The ignorant is who was ignorant to his matter.

572. Rewarding the good deed with evil, that is infidelity.

573. The one in hurry is mistaken even though he might be a king.

574. The mean is ungrateful to the favours.

575. Anger is evil, if you obeyed it, it shall destroy.

576. Getting back to the sin that is insisting.

577. The strange one who has no beloved ones.

578. The ignorant is he who was tricked by the goals.

579. Exaggerating in jokes is stupidity.

580. When someone likes himself, that is stupidity.

581. Greed for food is one of the bad manners.

582. Lying leads to hypocrisy.

583. Arguing in faith corrupts the certainty.

584. Formality is a character of the hypocrites.

585. The ordered matters are disturbed by arguing.

586. The hearer of the slander is like the one saying it.

587. Tricking who trusts you is infidelity.

588. Slandering is the food of the dogs of hell.

589. Showing poverty brings poverty. [Meaning pretending to be poor].

590. Promise is a sickness, and its cure is to fulfil it.

591. Envy is the greatest flaw of Iblees (Lucifer, Satan).

592. Pride is the greatest trap of Iblees.

593. Misery falls in many flaws.

594. Greed of food is a collector for the shameful traits.

595. The ignorant is dead though he is alive.

596. Lying is the corruption of everything.

597. The ignorant is he who ignored his level.

598. Boredom corrupts the brotherhood.

599. Misery lowers the courage down.

600. Injustice kills its owner.

601. The untruthfulness slides with its rider.

602. The life is the place of trials.

603. Greed humiliates the prince.

604. The winner with evil is a loser.

605. The desires are the ride of disturbance.

606. Envy creates the hope.

607. Begging is the key to poverty.

608. The envious shall not dominate.

609. The doubtful has no faith.

610. The wicked has no doubts. [No doubts concerning his honour].

611. The one who likes himself, has no mind.

612. Ignorance brings ego.

613. Insisting is the most devilish of opinions.

614. Ignorance the most harmful enemy.

615. The envy disturbs the living.

616. The anger is the boat of recklessness.

617. Injustice is the lost of people.

618. Insistence is the title of damage.

619. The greed (for food) erupts the anger.

620. Aggression reveals destruction.

621. Injustice reveals the hell.

622. Sinning prevents the answers (of prayers).

623. Recklessness disturbs the living.

624. Pride of the favour corrupts the favour.

625. The envious is always sick.

626. The miser is always humiliated.

627. Misery produces hatred.

628. Greed is an eternal enslavement.

629. Lying reveals the hatred.

630. Lying lowers the human.

631. Hypocrisy corrupts the faith.

632. Hypocrisy is the twin of infidelity.

633. Treachery is equal to lying.

634. Liking oneself corrupts the mind.

ADAGES OF IMAM ALI (PUH) IN SATIRIZING THE LIFE

1. Life is made for others and not for itself.

2. It is for the low level of this life that Allah is disobeyed only in it, and nothing can be gotten from Him except by leaving it.

3. The bitterness of this life is the sweetness of the after-life, and the sweetness of this life is the bitterness of the after-life.

4. Life humiliates.

5. Life is the market of losing.

6. Life is the place of miserable ones.

7. Life is full of troubles, frequent with adversities and disasters.

8. The little of this life corrupts the faith.

9. Life gives you up.

10. Faith for the after-life is not useful with love for this life.

11. Being happy about life is a stupidity.

12. Life will end.

13. Life do not protect who takes refuge unto her.

14. Life is the deal of the tricked, and the human being is tricked by it.

15. The little of this life is enough, and too much of it would kill.

16. Life is divorced by the smart people.

17. The companion of the life is a target for adversities and changes.

18. Who turns away from life it shall come him by force.

19. Who is not satisfied with Allah away from this life, then he has no religion.

20. Who was gave life away then he did not miss it.

21. Who depends on this life, then he is a troublesome banned man.

22. Who fights against life shall be dead.

23. Who spends too much asking for life shall die poor.

24. Who races against life it shall go before him.

25. Who works for this life then had lost.

26. Who sells his after-life for his life then he had lost both.

27. If the people of this life understood, then this life would be destroyed.

28. How many are there who were sure about this life and then got troubled.

29. Who built his life then corrupted his after-life.

30. How many are there of wise men who corrupted their ends.

31. Who takes care of life is doomed.

32. Everything in this life shall over.

33. Who was tricked by this life, then shell be clogged with hopes.

34. How many are there who were trusting this life until it killed them.

35. Who was satisfied about this life, then missed the after-life.

36. Troubles were linked to the love of this life.

37. In leaving life, lies the path of success.

38. The ego of life kills.

39. In this life, the rest of the troubled ones.

40. The goal of this life is to end.

41. The divorce of this life is the dowry of paradise.

42. The health of this life is full of sickness, and its lusts are full of pains.

43. Asking for life, that is the head of disturbance.

44. The fixation of the after-life is to deny the life.

45. The most devilish of disturbances, the love of life.

46. The happiness of this life is ego, and its enjoyment is to end.

47. The ornaments of life corrupts the weak minds.

48. The reason for the corruption of mind is the love of this life.

49. The head of beasts, falling in love with this life.

50. Mentioning life is the sickest illness.

51. Mixing up with the children of this life, that is the head of adversity and the corruption of piety.

52. The love of life is the head of every sin.

53. The sweetness of this life is the bitterness of the after-life and the bad end.

54. The neighbour of this life is in war, and its abundance is troubled.

55. The love of life is the head for every disturbance, and the origin for every adversity.

56. The love of life is the reason for disturbances.

57. The love of life reveals the greed.

58. Bad is the place of life.

59. By death, life is ended.

60. The greatest adversities and troublesome times is the love of this life.

61. The smartest of people is he who refuses his life.

62. The best garment for this life is to reject it.

63. The greatest sin, the love of life.

64. The best of worshipping is to give life up.

65. Life is a place full of dangers.

ADAGES OF IMAM ALI (PUH) IN CALLING FOR THE AFTER-LIFE

1. Remember the stopping of the lusts and the remaining of the consequences.

2. Who remembers how far the travel is shall be make himself ready.

3. Leaving is near.

4. The breath of the man is his steps to his end.

5. The people of this life are like riders taken away while they are asleep.

6. The wise man should give for his after-life and build the place of his living.

7. The beauty of lust do not satisfy the torture of hell.

8. No remains of age with the continuation of day and night.

9. No absent is closer than death.

10. Life is the passage to the after-life.

11. Trusting the life is a stupidity.

12. Age is made of counted breaths.

13. Nothing is more truthful like death.

14. His wishes are granted, who works for the lasting place.

15. No comer is closer than death.

16. Life is a passage and the after-life is a place of settlement.

17. How close is the living to the dead, for soon it will follow.

18. Who asks for death is not spared.

19. It is a trouble to corrupt the after-life.

20. For everything living there is a death.

21. Who remembers how long is the way of travel, should be ready.

22. Who does not prefer the after-life upon this life, he is then mindless.

23. Everything from the after-life is eternal.

24. How is he safe from death who asks for it?

25. Who sees death with the eye of his true belief, he shall see it soon.

26. In working for the after-life, success is reached.

27. Who is certain of the end, shall take a lot of supplies.

28. The absent death is the the one waiting with rights, and the closest comer.

29. I am amazed for an ignorant and death is running after him.

30. The goal of the after-life is eternity.

31. He is busy away from paradise who has the hell in front of him.

32. Mentioning the after-life is a medicine and a cure.

33. Mentioning death, lessens the reasons for life.

34. The sweetness of the after-life removes the bitterness of troubles in this life.

35. The rewards of the after-life makes you forget the tiresome times of life.

36. Your stay is to end, and your end is to be eternal.

37. Start before the coming of the awaited absent.

38. Start before the take of Almight.

39. Start before the fear (of death) and letting go of the soul.

40. Start with your richness before your poverty and with your life before your death.

41. If mourners come to you a lot, the mourners shall mourn you.

42. It is an adversity to corrupt the after-life.

43. The one who wins a lot is he who buys the after-life with his life.

44. Where are the giants (Amaliks) and the sons of the giants.

45. Where are the tyrants and the sons of tyrants.

46. Where are those who built the camps and cities.

47. Where are they who said "who is mightier than us, and more numerous."

48. Where is he, who strived and worked, and prepared and collected.

50. Where is he who built and constructed, and spread and prepared (the roads), and collected and counted. [Wrong numbering in the book itself, ignore it].

51. Where is he who fortified and assured, and ornamented and upholstered.

52. Where are they who were longer than you in lives and made more traces (than you).

53. Where are the kings and kisras. [Kisra is the title of kingship in Persia in old days].

54. Where are Bani Al-Asfar (tribe) and the pharaohs. [Bani Al-Asfar, Arabic for: Children of the yellow one, it might be a title for the Romans and/or Byzantines, for at that time the Byzantines were already driven out of Arabia].

55. Where are those who owned the far lands in the world.

56. Where are they who enslaved the nations.

57. Is there anyone who awakes from his sleep before the time of his death.

58. Is there anyone who gets cautious from his ignorance before his time is over.

59. Is there anyone who is ready to meet his God before letting go of his soul.

60. Is there anyone who gets the supplies for his after-life before the time of his leaving.

61. Is there anyone who repents for his sins before the arrival of his death.

62. Be prepared for death for its shade hare hovering over you all.

63. Make your determination and seriousness for your after-life.

64. Paradise is the best end, and the hell is the most devilish of settlements.

HIS ADAGES (PUH) ABOUT RICHNESS, POVERTY AND MONEY

1. Richness and poverty shall be after being judges by Allah.

2. Poverty is the grand death.

3. The most honourable richness is to leave the pride (about it).

4. May there be a poor man who is richer than every rich man.

5. The richest richness, the satisfaction (about what one has).

6. No richness with the bad planning.

7. Money is the amusement of the heirs.

8. Richness makes authority for someone other than the master.

9. Got rich who was satisfied about destiny.

10. No poverty with good planning.

11. He is not poor who has a good understanding.

12. A person does not dignify himself until he humiliates his money.

13. Who depended on Allah is in no need for His slaves.

14. No pride in money except with generosity.

15. He is not given money who does not spend it.

16. Fortune is not gained by wishing.

17. He did not gain money who does not fix it.

18. No richness with squandering.

19. No poverty with chastity.

20. No poverty for a wise man.

21. A rich man is not saved from death for the money he has.

22. Be satisfied and you shall be rich.

23. How many a rich man are there that are useless.

24. No richness for an ignorant.

25. He shall not be poor who is a monk.

26. Every miser is a poor man.

27. Satisfaction (about what one has) is linked to richness.

28. The damage of poverty is safer than the evil of richness.

29. The most devilish of money is what brings the curses.

30. The deeds of money shall vanish when it (money) vanishes.

31. The bad planning is the key to poverty.

32. The reason for poverty, squandering.

33. The zakat (almsgiving) of money, is to give. [Zakat in general means something that purifies the money].

34. May there be a rich man who is poorer than the poor.

35. May there be a poverty that gains the richness.

36. May there be a richness that brings the poverty.

37. The dirham of the poor man is beloved to Allah more than the dinar of the rich man. [A dinar is equal to 10 dirhams].

38. The best richness is the richness of the soul.

39. The love of money worsens the end.

POTIC ADAGES

1. People are equal in shapes *** Their father is Adam and the mother is Eve.

2. Verily the mothers of people are containers *** kept away and for lineages there are fathers.

3. And if they have in their origin some honour *** that makes them proud, then mud and water.

4. Virtue is verily for the people of wisdom for they *** are guided and guiders for anyone asking.

5. And the value of a person is what he does best *** and the ignorant ones for the wise are enemies.

6. Thus stand up with a wisdom, and do not ask for a change *** For people are dead, and wise men are alive.

7. And may there be a brother that I did his right *** but no loyalty lasts for him.

8. Every affection shall be clear for Allah's sake *** but wickedness is not clear with brotherhood.

9. And every injury has a medicine *** and the bad manner has no medicine.

10. And luxury is not lasting forever *** and so is the poverty shall not.

11. If I denied a promise from a loved one *** the in myself lies generosity and shyness.

12. And the smart wise kid is he who when *** life becomes treacherous, he is not sorry for it.

13. If destiny decided a matter upon you *** then nothing shall solve it except of destiny itself.

14. Take a little for everything *** from this life has an end.

15. Be aware of this life for its field *** is a place of ending and not settling.

16. And living is not done by wishing *** but drop your bucket with the buckets.

17. Who died and rested is not a dead *** but the dead is the dead amongst the living.

18. And how many those who run after wealth but did not get it *** and others did not run but got wealthy.

19. Your life is counted breaths, every time *** a breath goes away, a part of you is taken.

20. By your life, a human is measured only by his religion *** so do not leave piety depending on ancestry.

21. For Islam raised Salman of Persia *** and paganism put down the master, Abu Lahab. [Salman is a companion of the prophet Mohammed (puh) and was from Persia. They say his real name was something else other than Salman and the prophet himself called named him Salman, and the prophet himself said about him "Salman is one of us, folk of the House," meaning he is considered to be a member of the holy family of the prophet (puh) although he was a stranger. He was originally raised in a fire-worshipping community and converted to a Christian monotheist, until the raise of Islam when he became a muslim and a companion for prophet Mohammed (puh). Abu Lahab is the prophet's own uncle who opposed his nephew and harmed him in the beginning of Islam].

22. I taught myself the manners and did not find for it *** except of fearing God to be the lesson.

23. If it is made of silver, your speech O *** soul, then silence is verily made of gold.

24. And all the troubles when they arrive *** then linked to them a close by relief.

25. If this life was generous to you then be generous with it *** over the people, for it flips over and over.

26. Cover your brother over his flaws *** and veil and cover his sins.

27. And be patient for the injustice of the silly *** and for the time and its matters.

28. But the fortunes are a luck and a destiny *** by the favour of a King and not by a trick of a seeker.

29. Beauty is not by garments that ornament us *** but beauty is the beauty of mind and manners.

30. The orphan is not whose father is dead *** orphan is verily who is orphan of wisdom and manners.

31. Do not seek a living by humiliation *** and avoid yourself from seeking the low.

32. The flaws of a man are covered by his growing money *** believed in what he says while he was lying.

33. And puts down the mind of the wise because of lack of money *** people make him stupid while he is a smart one.

34. And patience in the adversities is hard *** but harder is to miss the rewards.

35. And everything sought after is near by *** and death is closer than everything.

36. Wear the cloak of patience at the time of adversities *** and you shall gain from patience, the good endings.

37. And be a friend for kindness in every scene *** for kindness is the best companion and friend.

38. And be a saver for the covenant of the friend and a protector *** and you shall taste from the complete protection the clearest drinks.

39. And be grateful to Allah for every favour *** and He shall reward you for it with many gifts.

40. And be a seeker for the fortune from the doors of Halal (law) *** thus fortune will be multiplied for you from all the sides.

41. And save your face's water (dignity) and do not give it *** and do not ask the low ones for a favour.

42. And be hospitable for the friend whenever he comes *** to you, with true affection that is required from you.

43. O son, fortune is taken care of *** thus you must seek the beautiful.

44. Do not let the money be your own gain *** and the protection of your God make it as a gain.

45. The Lord took care of giving every living *** and money is borrowed, that comes and goes.

46. Fortune is faster than the looking of an observer *** for a road, to a human when he is crossing.

47. And lower your wings for the friend and be for him *** as a father who bends down to his children.

48. And the guest be hospitable for him as much as you can *** until he seems like a heir with some connection.

49. And let your friend be, who when you be a friend of him *** he keeps the friendship and protects for you.

50. And save your friend in all situations *** and go along with someone who does not lie.

51. And desert the liar and his closeness and his sides *** for a liar shall make dirty who goes with him.

52. Thus, for the obedience of Allah hold on and win *** verily the pious is the beautiful and the respected.

53. And work for his obedience and you shall gain His satisfaction *** for the obedient to his God shall be a close one.

54. And be satisfied for satisfaction bears relaxation *** and being despaired of what was missed that is what is required.

55. And if you saw the friend with flattery *** then he is the enemy and his right is to be avoided.

56. No good is there in the affection of a flatterer *** with sweet tongue and a fire in the heart.

57. Verily the wealthy of men is dignified *** and you see what he has is sought after and he is feared.

58. And poverty is bad for men for it *** can lower down the courageous, the smartest and the noblest.

59. And lower down your wing for all the relatives *** with humility and allow them if they have mistaken.

60. And let go of the liar and do not let him be your friend *** for a liar is the worst of friends to be.

61. And let go of the envious even if he was clear for you *** get him away from your sight and not begotten.

62. And weigh the talk if you spoke and do not be *** blabbering in every gathering you would speak.

63. And save your tongue be aware of what it says *** for a person might be safe and endangered by it.

64. And the secret you shall keep and never say *** for it is the prisoner with you if not taken away.

65. Do not be a miser for misery do not add up *** to the fortune but tires the miser and troubles him.

66. Keep the trust and avoid the treachery *** and be just and do not wrong thus you gained the sweet.

67. And be aware from the wronged one for a direct arrow *** and know that his prayer has no veil (to Allah).

68. O builder of your high palace, make it low *** for you (will be) living in the ruined grave.

69. Life is but a field *** life has no stability.

70. Life is but like a house *** woven by the spider.

71. Thus death is true and dying is but a sip *** that comes to you so start up the charity.

72. Passion is a bless and patience is happiness *** thus be patient in a matter and success is yours.

73. The friend of my enemy enters my enmity *** and I am for whom befriended the friend, a friend.

74. And do not delay doing the good for tomorrow *** maybe tomorrow will come and you are missing.

75. The preacher do not fix the heart of someone *** who Allah did not decide to guide.

76. And the happiness do not last for people *** and the bad luck is erased by nights of the good luck.

77. If the kid went up to the high places *** then the least important to be missed is the sweet sleep.

78. The thoughts of men are about many things *** and my thought in this life is to get a helping friend.

79. For death in us there are correct arrows *** if one today was missed by an arrow he shall not tomorrow.

80. Be sure to be good to both your parents *** and goodness to the close ones and the far.

81. And by Allah, take the refuge and do not seek someone else *** and do not be neglectful to His favours.

82. And compete in giving money to gain the highness *** by a determination of a good-mannered and glorified one.

83. You hope in this life for long and you do not know *** if night comes would you live until dawn.

84. For how many are there of healthy ones died for no sickness *** and how many are there of sick ones that lived from time to time.

85. And how many are there of kids that by night and morning he is safe *** and his coffins are woven but he does not know.

86. O seeker of happiness in life without disturbance *** you asked for non-existent thus despair from winning.

87. In cowardice lies shame and in courage lies honour *** and who escapes shall not be safe from destiny.

88. The pleasure disappears from who got his lust *** by the Haram, and remains the sin and the shame.

89. This life for its seeker is *** but tiredness and he does not know.

90. When it comes it makes him busy from his faith *** or when it goes away it makes him busy with poverty.

91. I found out and days bear an experience *** for patience there is an ending that is good in consequence.

92. There are few who work on their requests *** and took the patience along then surely they are winners.

93. There is a habit for me in every day *** when it is bad then patience and when it is good then giving thanks.

94. Be patient a little for after the hardness comes easiness *** and every matter has a timing and planning.

95. And for the Dominant in our cases He has a view *** and above our planning, for Allah there is a planning.

96. Knowing Allah is the sum of giving thanks *** and being ignorant to Allah that is the sun of infidelity.

97. If someone did not live with wisdom is a dead *** and until the time of resurrection has no resurrection.

98. Induce your sons to learn the manners when young *** so that your eyes would be happy with them when you are old.

99. And the likes of summation of manners *** at the young age is like engraving on stones.

100. Verily, when the feet of the well-mannered slides a bit *** he will fall down to the beds of silk and happiness.

101. If you do not know and did not ask *** about wisdom then who knows if you are ignorant while you do not know.

102. And the shame is to be honourable amongst the people *** and at the time of war you are an escaper.

103. Did you not see that poverty is hoped to be richness *** and wealth is feared to be down into poverty?

104. For money covers all the flaws *** and in poverty lies humility and lowering down.

105. Take care of the brothers of clearness for they are *** pillars when you ask for their help and supportive.

106. And it is not much to have one thousand friends and companions *** and one enemy is even too much.

107. Verily, young people are excused if they did not know *** and any excuse is not accepted from an old man.

108. If the life bit you then wait for a relief *** for it shall come the one waiting for it.

109. And take it easy for the matters *** are in the palm of God with their destiny.

110. Who goes along with life shall curse it companionship *** and shall take from its nice times and the hard ones.

111. How many a bite that brought death to the biter *** like a seed of wheat that broke the neck of a little bird.

112. Then say for who cursed the troubles of time *** you wronged the time but curse the humans.

113. All the benefits of this life are just ego *** and no happiness lasts for a happy one.

114. Wisdom is an ornament thus be an owner for it *** and be a seeker for it as long as you live.

115. And be a monk that was fed faith and pious *** gaining religion and preying for wisdom.

116. And know, may you be guided, that wisdom is the best relief *** that became easy going for its seeker.

117. And silence makes clear thoughts of the kid *** and he might be a silly one of ill-manners.

118. And let go of joking for there may be a spell of a joker *** that brought to you badness not avoidable.

119. Satisfaction provided me with every honour *** is there any honour more honourable than satisfaction.

120. Let go of caution for this life *** and do not be greedy about living.

121. And do not gather all the money *** for you do not know for whom you do it.

122. For fortune is divided *** and the hard doing of a man is not useful.

123. Poor he is every one that becomes greedy *** and rich is he who gets satisfied.

124. O owner of the sin do not despair *** for God is passionate and passionate.

125. If you seek the level of the nobles *** then do the good and be just.

126. And ask for fortune from the Merciful's gift *** for there is no giver except of Allah.

127. He did not compensate, who begs, by his begging *** even if he got what he wants by begging.

128. If life is considered valuable *** then the reward of Allah is higher and nobler.

129. And if the fortunes are by luck and divided *** then being less careful about gaining is more beautiful.

130. And if money is collected to be left over *** then why with such left over a man becomes a miser.

131. And if the bodies are made to be dead *** then the killing of someone by a sword for Allah is better.

132. And no goodness there is in a promise if it was a lie *** and no goodness is there in a saying without an action.

133. If you have a wisdom and without a mind *** then you are like a sandal that has no foot.

134. And if you are an owner of a mind but not a wise man *** then you are like a foot that has no sandal.

135. Life is but like a shade that will go away *** or like a guest that stayed at night then travelled.

136. Give life and it will be driven to you *** is not the destiny of that one is to end?

137. I will be satisfied as long as I live with my day's supply *** and shall not seek the abundance of money.

138. Your happiness in this life is an ego and a regret *** and your living in this life is impossible and false.

139. Take supplies from this life for you will be leaving *** and start for death shall be revealed, no doubt.

140. I do not accept all life with a pride *** and I do not buy the high levels with humility.

141. A straight seeker is not like *** who was a guider and humiliated.

142. The kid dies from a falling of his tongue *** and the human does not die from falling of the foot.

143. Death is verily a sip that will be taken *** do not be afraid and pack for travelling.

144. Be patient for the great event *** and cure your injuries with beautiful patience.

145. And do not be scared if you had a hardship *** for you were in ease in a long time.

146. And do not despair for desperation is infidelity *** and may Allah make you satisfied from a little.

147. I saw the hardship followed by easiness *** and the saying of Allah is the most true of all sayings.

148. And neglecting the favour is a call for *** removing it and giving thanks make it last.

149. If this wisdom is to be taken by wishes *** then no ignorant people will be left in this life.

150. Work hard and do not be lazy or ignorant *** for the regretful end is for the lazy one.

151. And I tasted the bitterness of things *** and no taste is more bitter than begging.

152. And did not see in troubles a more dangerous thing *** and harder than being enemy to the men.

153. The rich is the rich one with his heart *** the rich is not the rich one with his money.

154. And so is the generous, he is the generous with his manners *** and the generous is not the one of high tribe and family.

155. And so the scholar is the scholar with his conditions *** and not the scholar of speech and sayings.

156. You are loved by some people when turned into wealthy one *** and every wealthy man is glorified in the eyes.

157. Take care of three and keep them a secret *** your bravery and your wisdom and your money.

158. Do not be afraid of being thin for may be *** the fat one is slain and the thin is left over.

159. And make your heart for humility as a house *** for humility for a noble one is beautiful.

160. If you are given the matters of some people in one night *** then you should know you are responsible for them.

161. And if you carried to the graves a funeral *** then know that you are after that shall be carried.

162. O you who got busy with his life *** you got tricked by the long hopes.

163. Death comes suddenly *** and the grave is the box of the deeds.

164. Protect the soul and let it do what makes it pretty *** and you shall live peacefully and sayings about you shall be so.

165. And if the fortune of today got narrowed then wait until tomorrow *** may the troubles of time get away from you.

166. The man of a rich soul is glorified though with less money *** and the man of money richness gets rich though he is humiliated.

167. And no goodness in the affection of a colourful person *** when the winds change direction he goes where it goes.

168. For how many a brothers are there when you count them *** but in times of troubles they are but a little.

169. For money shall end soon *** and wisdom shall remain with no end.

170. And if you need something from a generous one *** then meeting him is enough and to greet as well.

171. Do not wrong if you are able *** for injustice's end is to regret.

172. Your eyes sleep and the wronged one is awake *** prays upon you and the eyes of Allah did not sleep.

173. If you are in a favour then care about it *** for the sins takes away the favours.

174. And if you give your soul what it desires *** for when it is satisfied, regret is revealed.

175. If a matter is completed and its flaw appeared *** then expect a destruction when they say it is done.

176. Live as a generous or a miser if you like *** sadness is a must in this life.

177. Your life is attached to sadness *** life is not passed without sadness.

178. Life does not come one day *** with happiness and completes it.

179. Do not be for life with an injured heart *** for fortune is taken care of by Allah the Generous.

180. Be with a rich soul and be satisfied with the little *** die and do not ask for something from a mean.

181. For the injury is the injury of the tongue you know *** and may there be a saying that drops with blood.

182. Do not leave a secret except with an honourable one *** and the secret with the honourables is kept.

183. By Allah wronging is an ill luck bringer *** and the sinner is the unjust.

184. Avoid the company of the mean ones *** and gather around the honourables, sons of the honourables.

185. And do not trust life for one day *** for life is a separated system.

186. And be for wisdom, a seeker and searcher *** and debate in what is allowed and what is not.

187. And if a friend betrayed you do not betray him *** and keep his saving and his cursing.

188. And do not have a grudge against the brothers *** and be a forgiver thus you are safe from sins.

189. A life that turns with its people *** in every day for two times.

190. Do not obey for a creature for greed *** for this is a weakness for you in faith.

191. And ask Allah for what He has in His keepings *** for His command is done between Kaf and Nuun. [Kaf and Nuun are two letters in Arabic and they form the word "Kun" which means "Be!," the imperative form of "to be"].

192. How good is religion and life when they gather *** may Allah never bless a life without a religion.

193. And if life betrayed you then be patient *** and be for the sake of Allah, of good manners.

194. And if the Generous One give you a gift *** then with giving thanks, let your tongue go.

195. Divorce this life for three times *** and ask for another wife for yourself.

196. The person is measured by a person *** when he walks with him.

197. The soul cried for life and it knows *** that safety is to leave what it has.

198. No house to live in for the man after death *** except of that one which he built before death.

199. Where are the kings that ruled *** until they drank from the cup of death?

200. Our money is for the heirs that we collect it *** and our houses for the ruins of time we are building.

201. How many cities in the horizon were built *** went to be ruins and death got closer to their people.

202. Do not blame the slaves (of Allah) for *** your fortune will come when you are allowed to.

203. Spread your wealth and protect your poverty *** that shall tire your interior without showing it.

204. May there be a day that made your cry *** and when you had been in another your cried for.

205. And how many are there for Allah of hidden gifts *** so hard to be understood even by the smart one.

206. How many of easy times that came after hardships *** that relieved the trouble of the sad heart.

207. And how many matters that hurt you in the morning *** and the happiness comes to you at night time.

208. Cure your soul with satisfaction or else *** it would ask from you over it necessities.

209. The soul is scared for being poor *** and poverty is better than a wealth that hovers over it.

210. The wealth of the soul is satisfaction, and if it did not accept *** then all what is on earth is not enough for it.

211. The honours are purified manners *** and faith is their first and mind is their second.

212. Your life is attached to anxiety *** life is not passed without worries.

MOST IMPORTANT SOURCES OF THE BOOK

- Nahjul Balaaghah [Path of Eloquence], chapter of short adages, collected by Al-Shareef Al-Radhey.
- Ghorar Al-Hikam wa-Dorar Al-Kalim [The first of adages, and the pearls of speeches], collected by Al-Amidi.
- Al-Diwaan [poetry collection] reported to imam Ali (puh).
- Nahjul-Balaaghah Al-Thaani [The second Path of Eloquence], collected by sheikh Jafar Al-Ha'iri.
- In addition, some books that contained some of his adages (puh).

www.ingramcontent.com/pod-product-compliance
Lightning Source LLC
Chambersburg PA
CBHW051548010526
44118CB00022B/2621